Rick Steves'
EUROPEAN EASTER

Rick Steves
and Gene Openshaw

TABLE OF CONTENTS

INTRODUCTION

EUROPE IS MY FAVORITE PLACE to travel, with its charming mix of people, history, and traditions. And Easter is a time when these rich traditions come to the forefront. Every country, every village, every family has its own way of observing the Easter season—ranging from religious to raucous, from fasting to feasting, from chocolate eggs to lamb-gut stew. These fascinating cultural differences make Easter a season of mystery, magic, and just plain fun.

For Christians, Easter celebrates the central Christian event—Christ's suffering, Crucifixion, and Resurrection. This is the cornerstone of the Christian faith: that God gave his son to live on Earth among us to empathize with our mortal experience and share his Father's message with us. The life of Jesus culminated on the cross, where he died to save humankind from sin and bring the gift of salvation. Then he was resurrected, showing the promise of eternal life. For that reason,

Festive, fragrant, and dramatic floats fill the streets of Sevilla during Holy Week.

The Easter season is a rich mix of Christian and pagan rituals. Sights range from art celebrating the Resurrection of Jesus to gaily dressed characters symbolically plowing the soil to welcome life returning to the fields each spring.

Easter is the most sacred and thoughtful—and arguably most important—of Christian holidays. It's a time for quiet reflection and passionate ritual that swings from great sadness to great joy.

For students of history, Easter is an occasion to dig even deeper, to uncover the holiday's prehistoric origins. Just as European churches sit on the remains of pagan temples, the Easter story is founded on the remnants of pagan festivals. These lusty pre-Christian celebrations were incorporated into the Christian tradition, and many live on even today.

For kids, it's a time of magical fun, when adults take children's visions of the supernatural seriously. There are gift-giving rabbits, mysteriously hidden eggs, delightfully messy art projects, and candy, candy, candy. Adults get into the spirit, remembering their own childhoods. It's when friends gather, grandma and

With several generations gathered, this farm boy in Tuscany cracks open his chocolate egg, excited to discover a prize hiding inside.

grandpa come for dinner, and several generations can all enjoy specially-prepared foods, gifts, decorations, and precious time together.

Easter is an inherently joyous time, marking the end of winter and the arrival of spring. It's a time to celebrate a new start. Whether you believe in the Resurrection or just the return of flowers, sunshine, and the earth's bounty, it's the promise of new life.

Before we go further, I've got a few important disclaimers: The reality is that—as in America—not everyone in Europe makes a big deal of Easter. (Don't plan a special spring trip expecting to see festivities everywhere.) And as you read this book, you'll hear about all kinds of Easter traditions and customs, both religious and secular. I treat all of these as equally valid. The non-religious might scoff at the Bible story about a man who really died and came back to life. But taken on

Whether you celebrate the Resurrection or just the return of flowers after a long and cold winter, Easter is a time to enjoy the promise of new life.

faith, it's a rich story that helps believers understand the greatest gift ever given. When it comes to Easter customs, historians might have a different take on the exact origin story of the Easter Bunny or in which century a particular hymn became popular, but I'm writing more from a love of Easter than strict historical accuracy.

Be aware that many of the European traditions I feature are very local. Some are known only to a single village, or special only to a single family. It's hard to generalize about how "all" of Germany or "all" of Italy celebrates Easter. This book doesn't even try to do that. Instead, I focus on a few of the countries and customs I find most interesting. Many of my sources come from my travels—when locals tell me about their celebrations, I pass it along to you. While researching this book, I learned that nobody really knows much of anything for sure about the misty origins and meanings of many legends associated with Easter. If you're the type of person who needs everything to be proven fact . . . you're probably not reading this book.

Now, as you anticipate the arrival of another Easter, sit back and enjoy this book. We'll begin by traveling back in time to the origins of our Easter traditions. Then we'll travel through modern-day Europe, tracing the entire two-month-long celebration.

We'll start with the craziness of Carnival—from the masked balls of Venice, to monsters on the rampage in Slovenia, to a musical Mardi Gras in Switzerland.

Easter is preceded by Lent—40 days of sobriety and reflection. And Lent is preceded by the wildest party of the year—Carnival.

This is followed by 40 days and 40 nights of sobriety and reflection—the time known as Lent.

Then Easter time really heats up when we reach the Holy Week that leads up to Easter Sunday. We'll see thousands waving branches for Palm Sunday at the Vatican. Holy Week continues with special fervor in Spain, with all-night processions, passionate worship services, adoration of the Virgin Mary, and some provocative costumes.

We'll see how people prepare for the big event, including the secular traditions that accompany Easter—that world of kids, chocolate eggs, and home-cooked dishes.

Finally, we'll experience the joy of Easter Sunday as various cultures across Europe celebrate the Resurrection of Jesus along with the return of spring—each in their own way. Along the way, expect to find Easter customs that are both

foreign and familiar, offering new and different ways to celebrate the joy of the holiday. Whether your Easter is about bunnies or Bible stories, revelry or the Resurrection, it is a wondrous time.

Happy Easter!

Rick Steves

THE BIBLE STORY THROUGH ART

THE CHRISTIAN STORY OF EASTER

FOR CHRISTIANS, Easter is about the last days of Jesus of Nazareth—his death and Resurrection. These events transpired over a single week in history, around A.D. 33. That's when Jesus was arrested, tortured, and executed by the authorities. Then, on the third day after his death, Jesus came back to life and appeared to his followers.

These momentous events, collectively known as the Passion and the Resurrection, are known to history from several books of the Bible. The different authors of these books each relate slightly different details, but they basically tell the same story.

The central figure is Jesus of Nazareth (c. 4 B.C.–c. A.D. 33). He's also known to history as Jesus "Christ," a title meaning the messiah or chosen one. Born in Bethlehem to a mother named Mary, he was raised in Nazareth as a carpenter's son. Jesus was a Jew. He likely spent most of his life in (what is today's) Israel and Palestine. Back then, the region was part of the vast Roman Empire—ruled from Rome and administered locally by the Romans' Jewish subordinates.

Jesus formed a band of 12 disciples (a.k.a. apostles). He gained a reputation as an itinerant preacher and miracle worker—healing the sick, walking on water, turning water into wine, and more. He preached a message of loving your neighbor. He warned that the Kingdom of God was at hand, and would soon be established on earth. This part of his message sounded threatening and rebellious to the Roman and Jewish authorities, who took steps to have him arrested, tried, and killed. That final week of his life—the Passion, which led to his Resurrection—is what Easter is all about.

This remarkable story has helped shape Western history. For 2,000 years, the various episodes have been brought to life by many well-known artists, creating some of the world's masterpieces. Here's how those events are described in the Bible, and illustrated by timeless art.

Duccio, Christ's Entry into Jerusalem, *1308-11*

ENTRY INTO JERUSALEM

The Passion story begins the Sunday before Easter, as Jesus and his followers make a triumphal entry into the city of Jerusalem. The Bible says: "As they approached Jerusalem, a very large crowd cut branches and spread them on the road. They shouted joyfully: 'Hosanna! Hosanna in the highest!'"

PLOT TO KILL JESUS—
JUDAS AND THIRTY PIECES OF SILVER

On reaching Jerusalem, Jesus immediately alienated the authorities. He entered the temple and began driving out those who were buying and selling there. "My house will be called a house of prayer," he said, "but you have made it a den of thieves." He spoke ominously about the coming Kingdom of God. The chief priests and elders were troubled by how enthusiastically the common people were embracing Jesus. They plotted to arrest him. They offered Judas Iscariot, one of Jesus' 12 disciples, 30 pieces of silver to betray him. Judas agreed and they were delighted.

El Greco, Christ Driving the Traders from the Temple, *c. 1600*

THE LAST SUPPER

Leonardo da Vinci, The Last Supper, 1494-97

On the first day of Passover, as evening came, Jesus and the disciples gathered at the table. Jesus took bread, gave thanks, broke the bread and gave it to his disciples, saying, "Take and eat; this is my body." Then he took a cup, and said "Drink; this is my blood, which is poured out for the forgiveness of sins."

As they were eating, Jesus said, "Truly, one of you will betray me." They were all very concerned, and one by one they asked him, "Lord, is it I?"

Ugolino di Nerio, The Betrayal of Christ, *1325-28*

GETHSEMANE—ARREST, JUDAS, BETRAYAL

When they had sung a hymn, they went out to a place called Gethsemane. Jesus was deeply distressed, and his sweat was like drops of blood. He prayed, "Father, if it is possible, may this cup be taken from me. Yet not my will, but your will be done."

Just then, Judas appeared with a crowd armed with swords and clubs. Judas approached Jesus and said, "Greetings, teacher," and kissed him. The men seized Jesus. Then all of the disciples deserted him and ran away.

CHRIST BEFORE PILATE

They bound Jesus and took him to Pilate, the governor. When the chief priests accused Jesus of blasphemy, he made no reply. Pilate was amazed. He announced to the crowd: "I find no evidence against this man." But the chief priests stirred up the crowd. "Crucify him!" they shouted. "Crucify him!" Pilate took water and washed his hands, saying, "I am innocent of this man's blood." Then, hoping to placate the crowd, Pilate had Jesus whipped, and handed him over to be crucified.

Tintoretto, Christ Before Pilate, 1567

Flogging, Mocking, Crown of Thorns— The Way to Calvary

The soldiers spat on him, and struck him on the head with a staff. Then they stripped him and put a scarlet robe on him. They twisted together a crown of thorns and set it on his head. They put a staff in his right hand and knelt in front of him, and mocked him, saying "Hail, King of the Jews."

After they had mocked him, they led him out to be crucified.

Raphael, Christ Falls on the Way to Calvary, *1515-16*

Giotto, Crucifixion, c. 1303-5

CRUCIFIXION

Jesus carried his cross to the place called Golgotha, the Place of the Skull. And they crucified him.

   Above his head, they placed the written charge against him: "The King of the Jews." They crucified two robbers with him, one on his right and one on his left. They divided up his clothes by casting lots. Those who passed by shook their heads and mocked him. Even those crucified with him heaped insults on him. Jesus said, "Father, forgive them, for they know not what they do." At the sixth hour, darkness came over the whole land. And at the ninth hour Jesus cried out in a loud voice, "My God, my God, why have you forsaken me?" And when Jesus had cried out, he gave up his spirit and died.

Ugolino di Nerio, The Deposition, *1325-28*

DEPOSITION, LAMENTATION, BURIAL

As evening approached, they took down the body. Several of Jesus' female disciples were also there, watching from a distance. They wrapped the body in a clean linen cloth, and placed it in a tomb cut out of rock. Then they rolled a stone against the entrance of the tomb and went away. Pilate made the tomb secure by posting guards.

RESURRECTION

Very early on the first day of the week, just after sunrise, Mary Magdalene and the other women went to look at the tomb. They saw that the stone, which was very large, had been rolled away. They saw a young man. His countenance was brightly shining, and his clothes were white as snow. The guards were so afraid that they became incapacitated. "Don't be afraid," the young man said to the women. "You are looking for Jesus, who was crucified. He is not here. He has risen!"

Trembling and confused, the women fled from the tomb. Suddenly Jesus met them. "Do not be afraid," he said. They fell at his feet and worshipped him. Then Jesus said: "Go and tell my brothers they will see me." They told all these things to the disciples, but they did not believe the women, because their words seemed like nonsense.

Ugolino di Nerio, The Resurrection, 1325-28

Cima da Conegliano,
The Incredulity of St.
Thomas, *c. 1502-4*

Later Jesus appeared to the disciples as they were eating. They were startled and frightened, thinking they saw a ghost. "Why are you troubled?" Jesus said. "Look. It is I myself! Touch me and see." And he ate in their presence.

ASCENSION—CHRIST IN MAJESTY

Later, Jesus appeared again to his disciples. He led them outside. He lifted up his hands and blessed them. He said, "Go into all the world and preach the good news to all creation." While he was blessing them, he was taken up before their very eyes. He was taken up into heaven, where he sat on the right hand of God. He had told his disciples: "I am with you always."

THE ROOTS OF EASTER

THE PAGAN "EASTER"

WHILE CHRISTIANS have celebrated Easter for 2,000 years, the festival itself is much older. And it's no coincidence that it happens at the start of spring. For as long as people have shivered through a long cold winter, they have celebrated the arrival of spring.

Imagine you're living in Europe in prehistoric times. The bleakness of winter . . . the short days and long nights, the mist and rain, the barren fields, the hunger and the cold. You're at the mercy of nature, the fickle gods—Odin, Thor, and Freyja—and the elves, trolls, and Valkyries. In summer, the gods bring warmth, plants grow, and food is plentiful. Then it gets cold and dark, and the earth becomes frozen and forbidding.

Will better days ever return?

Druids and priests did their best to find out by tracking the course of the sun. They built impressive stone monuments to do this—in places like Stonehenge in England, Newgrange in Ireland, and hundreds of other rings of standing stones

The God Odin, from an Icelandic manuscript. Prehistoric people must have felt at the mercy of nature and the gods when winter came and the land died. Imagine their joy when life returned each spring.

Long before Christ, prehistoric societies set up stone circles like Stonehenge in England to function as celestial calendars. Druids would boogie on the vernal equinox, which marked the start of spring . . . and a party that came to be called Easter.

scattered around Europe. These stones were arranged to line up with the rising sun on important days, like the winter solstice (when the sun is at its lowest on the horizon) and the vernal equinox (marking the start of spring). Using these early astronomical observatories, prehistoric people could establish a crude calendar that offered some assurance that the sun would return again.

Imagine the comfort in knowing that the gods had not abandoned you. You might perform rituals passed down from your ancestors that gave you hope—asking the gods for the return of life, and thanking them when it comes. These customs and traditions—learned in childhood and passed on to the next generation—reminded everyone that the darkness of winter is always followed by life-giving spring. Just when you think that winter won't ever end, the clouds lift, and the sun breaks through.

What do you do? Throw a party! And slowly but surely, the earth revives. For the prehistoric people of Europe, this was their version of what came to be called "Easter."

Alfons Mucha, The Oath of Omladina under the Slavic Linden Tree, *1926. Pagans, completely oblivious to the Christian tradition of Easter, celebrated the return of life with each spring.*

EOSTRE AND THE EOSTRE BUNNY

The word "Easter" may come from the name "Eostre" or "Ostara." She was the Anglo-Saxon goddess of the dawn and of spring. In pre-Christian times, her feast day was celebrated on the first full moon following the spring equinox—the same calculation used today for the Christian Easter. Her festival was seen as a time of renewal, birth, and fertility.

Some cultural anthropologists have proposed that Eostre's legacy is more than just her name. According to Germanic mythology, the goddess' companion was the hare. Hares and rabbits—so prolific at reproduction—have long been a symbol of fertility and springtime.

Eostre, the Anglo-Saxon goddess of spring, traveled with a bunny (a very fertile duo).

From here, the mythology gets a little twisted. Apparently, Eostre had originally found an injured bird on the ground one winter. To save its life, she transformed it into the hare that became her sidekick. But the transformation was not complete and the hare retained the birdlike ability to lay eggs. In gratitude, the hare would decorate its eggs and leave them as gifts for Eostre.

Or so goes the mythology proposed by some scholars—and if you believe that, you probably also believe in the Easter Bunny.

THE CHRISTIAN REBRANDING

When Jesus died in Jerusalem (around A.D. 33), his life, death, and Resurrection were remembered by only a handful of followers. But gradually, the message of love that Jesus preached—the good news, or Gospel—spread into Europe. Despite severe persecution, Christianity began to win over the Jupiter-worshipping Romans, who ruled Western Europe. The first historical record of a Christian festival of Easter appears in the mid-second century.

When the Roman Emperor Constantine legalized the growing religion (c. A.D. 324), almost overnight the once-persecuted sect became a major religion in the Roman Empire. It was under Constantine that the early church leaders settled

Fears and superstitions filled each winter with anxiety—similar to our concern over the uncertainty of what happens after the winters of our lives.

on a standard date for Easter. By the fourth and fifth centuries, Christianity was firmly established throughout Europe—and so was the annual holiday of Easter.

But pagan Europe never fully went away.

Christians rebranded the earlier traditions to fit the story they wanted to tell. They wisely incorporated pre-Christian celebrations into their own calendar. They scheduled their religious festivals to coincide with seasonal events that had been observed since the dawn of time. The pagan festival of Saturn, which brought joy in the dead of winter, became the festive Christian holiday of Christmas. The pagan winter Bacchanal, a time of intrepid partying in the depth of the cold, became Carnival, which preceded Lent. Lent, which was tied to the late-winter season of scarcity—when nothing grew and the cupboards grew bare, became sanctified as a time of voluntary fasting and purification. And the celebration of Eostre, a pagan goddess representing how bleak winter blossoms into spring, became Easter—a celebration of how death is transformed into life with Christ's Resurrection.

For the next thousand years—the Middle Ages—Easter evolved into a mix of religious and pagan elements. Religious Christians celebrated Easter by devoutly reciting the Bible story of the Passion. This spoken liturgy soon turned into chants, which became songs accompanied by music. The priests wore special robes with symbolic meaning. Over time, these religious spectacles became more elaborate. The Passion story came to life, with people donning costumes to pose in tableaus as, for example, the devil, or Pilate washing his hands, or Judas betraying Christ. (The colorful Ommegang held in Brussels every year captures some of the pageantry of these medieval spectacles.) Over time, these liturgical tableaus blossomed into full-blown dramatic productions, with actors playing the roles. Spectators could watch the events of the Passion unfold before their eyes. These

Across Christendom, Passion Plays were performed as teaching aids to tell the biblical story of Easter.

have been passed down to us today as Passion Plays, which served as an inspiration for Shakespeare and others as they invented modern theater.

Meanwhile, along with the religious celebrations, medieval Europe retained its pagan customs. There were age-old fertility rites—singing and dancing, throwing flowers, gorging on sweets, and giving gifts. These originally celebrated the rebirth of nature with its bounty. Now they conveniently coincided with the Resurrection of Jesus. Even today, many Europeans gather around giant bonfires on Easter Eve to await the return of Jesus, just as their pagan forebears awaited the dawning of spring.

MODERN EASTER EVOLVES

Easter was transformed in the 1500s, when Catholics and Protestants parted ways during the tumultuous Reformation. In Catholic countries, the season remained firmly tied to tradition. Easter was (and still is) a bigger deal. People fasted strictly during Lent, and dutifully observed each day of Holy Week. The Virgin Mary, much adored in Catholic countries, was revered for her role in the Passion story. Catholic Easter services have remained elaborate productions—with incense, colorful robes, processions, and churches decorated with great artwork to inspire the faithful.

Meanwhile, Protestants during the 1500s and 1600s went through a phase where the trappings of Easter were stripped down to their basics. The simple, whitewashed churches of Protestant lands attest to how Protestant extremists purged their churches of artwork and showy luxury during a wave of violent iconoclasm.

But Easter survived.

Though Protestants downplayed the spectacle of Easter, they more than made up for it with other traditions. Lutherans of the Germanic lands in particular celebrated Easter with gusto. Many of our symbols of Easter—like the Easter Bunny

and Easter eggs—developed in Germany during the 1500s and 1600s. These traditions then made their way to America in the 1700s with German immigrants, such as the Pennsylvania Dutch.

By the 1800s, a new religion was seeping into Europe—secularism. But Easter survived that, too. Those who are only mildly religious make a point of attending church at least during Easter. And the traditions live on, even separate from their religious or pagan roots. Eggs, bunnies, candy, gift-giving, and general festiveness continue to mark Europe during Easter time. Easter has become increasingly commercial. With globalization, America's traditions—many of which were born in Europe—have been reinfused into the Old Country. American brands of candies and Easter Bunnies appear in European shop windows even in lands where the religious celebration is quite understated.

But—as we'll see—Europe still retains many of the old customs. Some of these traditions date back centuries—to medieval times, to pagan Rome, to the days of the earthly Jesus, and even to the dawn of man.

"WHY DOES EASTER FALL ON A DIFFERENT DATE EVERY YEAR?"

Easter is the first Sunday after the first full moon after the vernal equinox. Simple enough. But, since that date can fall anytime between March 22 and April 25, Easter is considered a "moveable feast," because the date moves from year to year. Why can't it be the same date every year? There are several reasons, and the explanation takes some unexpected turns, so follow me here:

Fundamentally, it's because the Easter holiday is so primal that it predates our modern scientific ways of keeping time. Its roots lie in the prehistoric peoples who used stone circles to chart their lives according to the passage of the sun and the

Easter is a moveable feast. Astronomers can explain why.

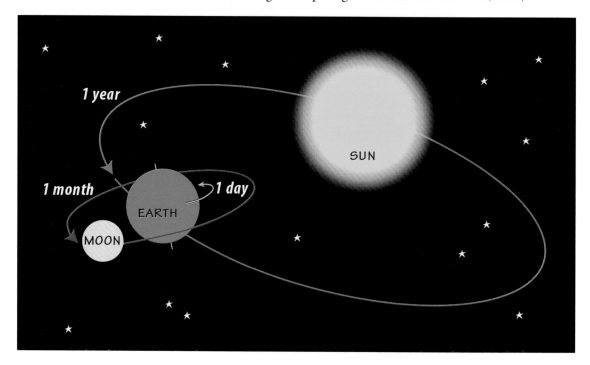

moon. Easter, with its pagan roots, was a spring festival tied to the return of the sun at the vernal equinox. The equinox is the day (around March 21st) when day and night are of equal length, and the long days of spring and summer are about to start.

So the date is set by the sun—but it's not that simple. The date of Easter is also tied to the moon. That's because Jesus' death (according to the Bible) happened during the Jewish holiday of Passover. And Passover begins at the first full moon after the equinox.

So the date of Easter is determined by both the sun and the moon. The problem is that those two celestial bodies don't move in sync with a third body, the revolving earth. (See the diagram on the facing page.) One "year" according to the solar calendar is 365 days, made up of 12 months (or "moons"). But a "year" made up of 12 full moons (which occur every 29.5 days) is only 354 days long. They don't line up—365 divided by 29.5 results in an unwieldy fraction of around 12.5 months in a year. So, if you're watching the heavens, using the sun and moon as your guide, the date of Easter will always be different year after year.

In A.D. 325, the early Christians gathered near Istanbul to settle the matter once and for all. This was the landmark Council of Nicea that also defined God as a Trinity of Father, Son, and Holy Spirit (as declared in the Nicene Creed still recited by many Christians today). The council firmly established the fixed date still used today for Easter—the Sunday after the first full moon after the vernal equinox. They reconciled the lunar calendar used by Jews (to establish the start of Passover) with the solar calendar so popular throughout the Roman Empire.

Finally, the date of Easter was settled. Or was it . . . ?

In fact, their date was only an approximation, determined not by trained astronomers actually observing the heavens, but by church scholars following a complex set of calculations passed down by tradition. The flaw was their starting point—the calendar popularized three centuries earlier by Julius Caesar. That Julian calendar defined a "year" as exactly 365 days. In fact, it takes 365.25 days (a "day" being one rotation of the earth) for the earth to complete its annual journey

around the sun. Because of this ¼-day of unaccounted-for time, as the centuries went on, Easter got farther and farther out of whack. By the 1500s, Easter was being celebrated in May—much later than its original purpose as a rite-of-spring festival tied to the equinox. Getting the date of Easter right was so important that it prompted drastic action that affects us today.

In 1582, Pope Gregory XIII scrapped the outmoded Julian calendar. He established the Gregorian calendar, adding a "leap year" every four years to account for the extra 0.25 day. That's the calendar we use today.

Finally, it was settled. Uh, not quite.

Eastern Orthodox Christians (in Greece, Russia, and many Slavic lands) celebrate Easter on a completely different day, usually a week or two later than the

West. That's because they still use the Julian calendar to establish Easter. Their definition of Easter is the same—the Sunday after the full moon after the equinox—but they date the equinox at the "March 21st" of the outmoded Julian calendar.

Similarly, even though Easter and Passover are forever linked in the original story of Jesus, today's Christians and Jews no longer celebrate Easter and Passover at the same time. Christians establish Easter by a solar calendar (Gregorian or Julian), while Jews base their calculations on their traditional lunar calendar.

So, when is Easter? The bottom line is this: Whichever calendar you use—solar or lunar, Gregorian or Julian, Christian or Jewish, Nicean-based or the calendar of modern science—Easter is and always will be a moveable feast. Easter is so important that, once this date has been decided upon, it determines all of the other related moveable feasts (e.g., Corpus Christi) in the liturgical calendar. (On the other hand, some saints' days and feasts are fixed to a specific date—no wonder the Vatican Museums have such a crazy list of closed days.) For devout Christians, many of their rituals and scripture readings throughout the year are decided by the all-important date of Easter.

THE EASTER SEASON

Easter is not a day, but a season.

According to the Christian calendar of feast days, Easter lasts over 100 days. It starts in the dead of winter, in late February, with the solemn church service of Ash Wednesday. This begins the 40 days of Lent, a period of fasting and reflection. It leads to Holy Week, which remembers the last week in Jesus' life. It culminates on Easter Sunday.

But it doesn't end there. The season called Eastertide continues another seven weeks. Easter Monday (the day after Easter) is a national holiday in many parts of Europe, a treasured family time for picnics, walks, and Easter leftovers. Forty

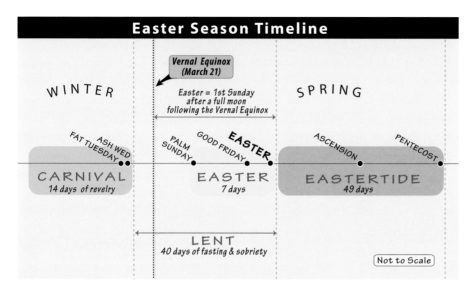

Easter Season Timeline

Vernal Equinox (March 21)

WINTER

Easter = 1st Sunday after a full moon following the Vernal Equinox

SPRING

FAT TUESDAY • ASH WED •

PALM SUNDAY • GOOD FRIDAY • **EASTER** •

ASCENSION • PENTECOST •

CARNIVAL
14 days of revelry

EASTER
7 days

EASTERTIDE
49 days

LENT
40 days of fasting & sobriety

Not to Scale

Easter is more than a single Sunday.

days after Easter comes Ascension Thursday, which celebrates the day Christ ascended to heaven. Eastertide culminates the 50th day after Easter on Pentecost. According to the Bible, this is the day that the Holy Spirit descended on the apostles—and, thus, the Church (as opposed to the ministry of Jesus himself) came into being. Pentecost marks the official end of the Easter season. After this, what's called "Ordinary Time" resumes in the Christian calendar.

Now, let's follow the entire Easter season—from Lent to Holy Week to Easter and beyond—seeing how it's observed in different countries. It all starts late in winter, with a big pre-Easter party known as Carnival.

CARNIVAL

Whether Carnival, Mardi Gras, or Fasching, It's a Party

The wild party that kicks off the reverent Easter season is known as Carnival. This late-February event is celebrated all around the world. In the States (especially New Orleans), we call it Mardi Gras. In Rio de Janeiro, it's Carnival (the world's biggest event). In Italy, they call it Carnevale. Germanic countries celebrate it as Karneval, or Fasching (in southern regions like Bavaria and Austria). It's called Fastnacht in Switzerland and Vastenavond in the Netherlands—both names mean "feast night." Specific towns might have a special name of their own for their particular local festival.

No matter where, Carnival is a time of craziness and excess before the seriousness, fasting, and abstinence of Lent, which leads into the reverence of Easter. The name probably comes from the fact that meat (or *carne* in Latin) was prohibited during Lent. So, "carne vale" meant "farewell to meat"—or in a larger sense, farewell to good food and the pleasures of the flesh. Carnival was one last carnal fling before the meager days ahead. The wildest celebrations tend to be in traditionally Catholic areas, where Lent has the most severe restrictions.

Carnival is probably rooted in pagan late-winter festivals, when people partied hardily to put on a brave face in the bleakest of seasons. By the fifth century, the Christian authorities realized that nobody was about to give up the biggest party of the year, and it became part of the Easter season.

Carnival is a time to do all the things restricted during Lent. It's a week (or more) of music, dancing, eating, drinking, and flirting. Partiers often wear masks and costumes. They decorate floats and parade through the streets, playing music and dancing amid a storm of confetti.

During Carnival, the traditional societal order is turned upside-down. Authority is challenged and rules are broken. A prince of fools might be given the key to the city, and a city council of faux-officials makes the rules. Joyous chaos reigns. This anti-authoritarian aspect of Carnival may date to medieval times, when

Across much of Europe, Carnival is a festive time of music, costumes, and parades designed to brighten the middle of a long and dreary winter.

society was ruled by an oppressive feudal hierarchy. Carnival served as a social safety-valve to let off steam—a time when poor peasants could swap places with their masters and be king for a day.

Preparations for Carnival start well before February. In Germanic lands, the craziness officially begins way back in November, when the Elferrat (Council of Eleven) gathers in front of the town hall, calls the meeting to order, dons their fool's caps, and—amid plenty of carousing—starts to plan the upcoming Carnival festivities.

Carnival itself generally begins one week before Ash Wednesday. With each succeeding day, the party picks up intensity until it culminates on Tuesday. This is variously called Shrove Tuesday, or Fat Tuesday, or, in French, Mardi Gras. It's the final blowout before the sudden sobriety of the next day, Ash Wednesday, when Lent begins.

Whatever the name, Carnival is often the biggest party of the year. Every place in Europe has a different way of celebrating, so let's look at some of the more interesting traditions. The most famous Carnival of all is in Venice.

VENICE'S CARNEVALE

Each winter, Carnevale casts a spell on Venetians and visitors alike. Several things make Venice's festival so unique—its long history, partiers in elaborate masks, and the one-of-a-kind location.

The island city of Venice—laced with canals and free of cars—is one of the world's greatest natural movie sets. It's the perfect backdrop for revelers in costumes making the scene. Any time of year, Venice is romantic: Gondolas glide gently down misty canals. Music plays nightly in St. Mark's Square, where people dance surrounded by fabled buildings of arches and domes. Venice is perfect for strolling down dark, narrow, peeling-plaster alleyways, and climbing to the top of a bridge to gaze down at your reflection in a quiet canal.

By February, all this atmosphere is just waiting for a party to arrive. Venice's Carnevale is not just a celebration, it's a piece of open-air theater.

Europe's "Fun City"

Venice has hosted Carnevale since at least the 13th century. Back then, Venice was Europe's wealthiest and most cosmopolitan city. Exotic luxury items from around the known world poured into this sea-trading city. Europeans traveled to Venice to enjoy spiced foods from Africa, silk clothes from Asia, and drink imported wine from glass goblets forged by Venetian artists. Carnevale became a worldwide phenomenon, attended by English barons, African Moors, Byzantine scholars, and Muslim sultans.

By the 1700s, even as Venice was in economic decline, it still had a reputation for luxury . . . now tinged with decadence. It was Europe's fun city—where aristocrats from across Europe traveled to do the kinds of things they were forbidden to do

During Carnival, what happens in Venice stays in Venice.

at home. They ate and drank too much, gambled at the licensed casinos, bought expensive glass chandeliers for their palaces back home, sat for souvenir portraits, and made visits to Venice's thousands of courtesans (i.e., prostitutes). The year-round indulgence kicked up an extra notch at Carnevale. Back then, Carnevale stretched from the day after Christmas until Lent. "Nowhere in Europe," wrote a visitor from France, "are there so many and such splendid *fêtes*, ceremonies, and public entertainments of all kinds as there are in Venice."

In 1798, Austrians took control of Venice and the party was over. Carnevale was banned. For two centuries, the city's party reputation slumbered. Then in the 1970s, Carnevale was once again revived (spearheaded by a mask making shop) and advertised to the world. Today, the festival thrives—it promotes a little more tourism, stokes the mask making business, and is a great excuse for a party.

The Mask

The key to Venice's decadence was always the mask. In former days, a mask allowed wealthy aristocrats (and even priests, friars, and bishops) to hide their identity as they indulged in what was taboo. In fact, masks were actually required by law in certain seedy establishments, to ensure that every sinner was equally

anonymous. During Carnevale, everyone wore masks. Frenchmen disguised as turbaned Muslims mingled with actual Turkish traders dressed as harlequins. Fake Barbary pirates fought playfully with skin-blackened "Moors." It was the time of year when all social classes partied as one, because (as one grateful visitor wrote) "the mask levels all distinctions."

Masks come in every variety—from animals to ogres to princesses to Cubist-style faces—but there are a few traditional masks that have been around for centuries. The classic getup for men is the *bautta*—a blank white mask that's always worn with a black three-cornered hat and a cowl. Also popular are stock characters from the lowbrow comedic theater called commedia dell' arte. The most famous of these is probably the wacky servant Harlequin, with his motley suit and simple Lone Ranger-type mask. You'll also see masks depicting the hypocritical plague doctor (with goggles and long nose), the country bumpkin Pulcinella (hook-nosed), and the pretty Columbina.

Masks are made with the simple technique of papier-mâché. You make a mold of clay, smear it with Vaseline (to make it easy to remove the finished mask), then create the mask by draping layers of paper and glue atop the clay mold. Thanks to the long tradition of Carnevale, Venice has become arguably the world's mask making capital.

Carnevale Today—Parties and Posers

Today, Venice's Carnevale draws thousands of visitors from around the world. The celebration does not include a big stereotypical Mardi-Gras-style parade. Rather, it's more a series of local parties.

Grand masked balls are a tradition in Venice.

First, there are the posers. Theatrical types (especially mimes from France) put on elaborate costumes and masks, and strike poses in public places. Suddenly, St. Mark's Square is populated with lords and ladies in silk gowns and masks, cavorting and gavotting, while tourists crowd around to snap photos. These people don't merely don a costume—they inhabit a role. They pose and gesture in character, moving slowly with pantomime-like motions. Of course, they choose the most striking of backdrops—under the arches of the lacy Doge's Palace, beside a weathered lion statue, or cruising in a decorated gondola.

Giacomo Casanova (1725-1798)

"I began to lead a life of complete freedom, caring for nothing except what pleased me."
—THE MEMOIRS OF GIACOMO CASANOVA

Casanova typifies the Venetian spirit of Carnevale that so entranced the rest of Europe. He was born along the Grand Canal, the son of an actor. He trained to be a priest, but was expelled for seducing nuns. He first made his name as a fiery violinist, playing for fancy parties in Venetian palazzos. Soon he was traveling all of Europe as a professional gambler and charmer—seducing noblewomen, dueling with fellow men of honor, and impressing nobles with his knowledge of Greek literature, religion, politics, and the female sex. He would later serve time in the Doge's Palace prison, accused of being a magician. By the time his memoirs were published (after his death), he'd cemented his reputation as a genial but cunning rake, rogue, and rapscallion . . . the very symbol of Venice's Carnevale.

As dusk falls, the back alleys come alive. Revelers—whether in fancy costumes or casual ones or none at all—crowd the pubs, enjoying *cicchetti* (toothpick appetizers) and *ombras* (small glasses) of cheap wine. They wander from pub to pub. They might stumble on an informal party erupting in a piazza or in someone's home that's open to almost anyone in a costume or a partying mood.

Meanwhile, more formal parties are underway. Fancy palazzos along the Grand Canal or on St. Mark's Square are rented out for the night. Some parties are limited to old friends, some are open to strangers (for a fee), and some are by invitation only. And some are very expensive, with thousand-dollar-a-plate spreads. (These often draw wealthy foreign business types, resulting in an awkward affair of stiff strangers. Personal experience tells me it doesn't take a lot of money to make a good party.)

Many Venetians have made it a tradition to gather together with their friends every Carnevale. It's a time to take a break from the stresses of their composed, controlled lives to let some fun and fantasy take over. The host makes sure their guests enter into a surreal world of fantasy and mirrors.

Caught up in Carnevale, it's easy to blink away the present and imagine you're back in Venice's glory days: Happy partygoers dance under candlelit chandeliers to Vivaldi's *Four Seasons*. Servants glide by with drinks and finger foods. The gentlemen wear powdered wigs, silk shirts with lacy sleeves, velvet coats, striped stockings, and shoes with big buckles. They carry snuffboxes with dirty pictures inside the lids. The ladies powder their hair and pile it high. And everyone wears or carries a mask on a stick to change identity in a second.

Now, as then, decadence rules the night and reality seems a distant dream. Carnevale is a time to say farewell to your old self. For at least one night, you're free to promenade, pose, and become someone you're not. And as it was centuries ago, what happens in Venice . . . stays in Venice.

Germanic Karneval— From "Elften elften" to Fat Tuesday

The Germanic countries really get into Carnival, especially in predominantly Catholic regions, such as Bavaria, Austria, and parts of Switzerland. The stereotype of Germans is of a people who are orderly, rational, and a little too buttoned down. But even if that were universally true (it isn't), the Germanic lands use Carnival as an occasion to bust out of that stuffy mold. Carnival here is a unique combination of order—long-range planning, elaborate themes, formal parades— and spontaneous zaniness. Unlike some parts of the world where Carnival can have a dicey edge, the Germans party hard in a safe and sane way . . . and quickly clean up their mess afterward.

The Germanic festival season (Karneval, Fasching, Fastnacht, or other local names) kicks off with a bang along the Rhine River Valley. The city of Cologne has hosted Karneval with exceptional zeal since 1341. It begins back in November, with their *"elften Elften um elf Uhr elf"* ceremonies (on the 11th day of the 11th month at the stroke of 11:11 in the morning), ushering in months of elaborate preparation.

People belong to Carnival clubs, who spend the winter intricately planning their partying—choosing their group's theme, creating and sewing their costumes, and constructing floats to enter in the Carnival parade. It's not all fun and games, though; many floats have a harsh edge of political satire, lampooning politicians and current events.

When February arrives, it's not just a single event, but a series spread out over a week. There's more than one masquerade ball. On one day of the Carnival week, women take control, and men make a point of wearing their least-favorite tie to the office, because the tradition is for women to ceremonially cut off men's ties. The week culminates the Monday before Lent with one of Germany's biggest street festivals—the Rosenmontag Parade, celebrated with floats and costumed characters, and broadcast throughout the country on live TV.

Luzern—Orderly Swiss Chaos

In Switzerland, the city of Luzern hosts the biggest Swiss Carnival. It's a unique event in Switzerland—a time when the normally reserved Swiss can cut loose with a burst of anarchy.

Luzern's specialty is masks. These aren't Venetian-style facial masks. Here masqueraders don huge, outsized heads made from papier-mâché. The goal is uniqueness and artistry, executed with the perfection of a Swiss watchmaker. Some masks are whimsical, but many have a darker edge, featuring horned devils and Gothic caricatures. There's a satirical political bite to the masks and floats that isn't normally seen in Swiss society, where everyone seems to know their place in the efficient order of things.

The other well-known element of Luzern's Carnival is music. It seems that each club has a marching band like you'd see in the military. But for Carnival, the emphasis is not on marching in lockstep, following a drum major. The music is purposely raucous, slightly out-of-tune, and with jazz-style improvisation that's intentionally a little rough around the edges.

The festivities begin one week before Ash Wednesday, when a big tree—the Guggerbaum—is erected on the main square. The next day—"Dirty Thursday"— is when the revelry begins. Each successive day has different parades (including a kiddie parade), a costume contest, and lots of drinking.

Day by day, the celebration builds. It culminates on the Fat Tuesday before Lent, with the main parade. The parade is big on provocative floats, outrageous masks, and loud, boisterous music—a traditional way to chase away the demons of winter with bizarre characters and noise.

The revelry starts well before sunrise. The driving beat of multiple parading bands wakes the city up like a mobile alarm clock. At first, things are pretty orderly. Everyone follows a set parade route, and spectators line up behind crowd barriers to watch. The marchers come in with their colorful floats, papier-mâché heads, and brass bands. Everyone politely applauds the creativity and artistry.

Carnival is big in Germany and Switzerland.

Then it gets weird. The parade splits up into smaller groups, and branches off the prescribed route. Soon revelers are wandering aimlessly down back alleys and generally taking over the whole city as the party goes on and on. You're walking along and suddenly, here comes a marching band—way too drunk, wearing crazy masks, improvising, and happily off-key. They stop into a bar to fuel up, then take the stage to spontaneously play more tunes. Then they're gone to the next pub.

The whole town gets caught up in the spirit. People clog the streets. Restaurants are packed. (Join me for a fondue and a beer?) Even five-star hotels open their doors and let the partying public celebrate inside.

As dusk settles in, all these dispersed marching bands somehow seem to find each other again. They merge together and reorganize for a long final parade. Musicians demonstrate that famous Swiss stamina, playing on and on. After the parade ends, the party continues, with the whole town dispersing once again—drinking, binge-eating, and dancing in the streets into the wee hours.

The thing is, all this unchecked craziness is somehow still very Swiss. The streets are never dangerous, just filled with a relaxed vibe of goodwill. No windows get broken and no one gets hurt. And at the end, the street-sweeping machine is there to make sure everyone wakes up the next morning to perfect Swiss cleanliness and order.

Slovenia—Primal and Unspoiled

Some of Europe's oldest and purest Easter traditions are found in the tiny, prosperous, and untouristed country of Slovenia.

Wedged between the Alps and the Adriatic, Slovenia feels both Germanic and Mediterranean, and its Easter traditions draw from both cultures. The country's snow-capped mountains, alpine villages, rolling countryside, and industrious people might make you think you're in Austria or Switzerland. On the other hand, as you enjoy seafood and a glass of wine while watching the sun set over the

Adriatic, you're soaking up the Mediterranean world. And the country's goulash of ethnic groups—Catholic Slovenes, Serbs, Croats, and Muslim Bosniaks—gives it an exotic, Slavic feel.

Slovenia is a charming, underrated land. The countryside is dotted with little barns to keep their hay dry, and with colorfully painted beehives—to help the bees find their way home. It's the birthplace of polka, and this art form is still bigger here than the Beatles or Kanye.

Because of the country's mountainous landscape, Slovenian villages tend to be small and isolated, and Easter traditions are very local. Each village, mountain valley, and cluster of farms has its own. Some customs are very old, with roots dating back to their pagan origins. They are deeply engrained in the village culture. These sometimes-bizarre customs can be hard for an outsider to understand, and, frankly, hard to explain.

But it's just this mix of elements that gives Slovenia some of Europe's most local and non-commercialized Easter traditions. And the people are some of the sweetest you'll find, very easygoing. Even when riled, the worst curse they can muster in their native tongue is "Three hundred hairy bears!"

The Kurents—Gotta Love 'em

Carnival time here is called Kurentovanje (koo-rent-oh-VAWN-yeh). Locals dress up in elaborate costumes and parade through the streets, celebrating the end of winter and heralding the arrival of spring. Each village in the area has its own particular costumes, cast of rowdy characters, and timeless rituals.

The star of the show is a big shaggy creature called Kurent. He's a fun-loving pagan Slavic god of hedonism—a Slovenian Bacchus—whose role is to scare off winter and usher in the joy of spring.

Kurentovanje all starts with the Kurent costume. This huggable beast has a bulky layer of shaggy sheepskin. He has a long red tongue, horns, a snout, whiskers, two red-ringed eyes, and wears red or green socks.

Traditionally, the participants (mostly young men) make their own Kurent costume. They work in secret, so their monster will be all the more startling when it's finally revealed. They use the stinkiest hides they can find, to make the beast smell as hideous as it looks and sounds.

Next, they attach five heavy cowbells to their waists. To finish it off, they carry a stick padded on one end with the skin of a spiny hedgehog. The whole getup can weigh 40 pounds or more.

The parade begins. Early in the morning, the men help each other get into their costumes and set off. Imagine a pack of a dozen or more hairy beasts rampaging through town, clanging their cowbells as loudly as possible. The noise is deafening. These horned monsters traverse the entire village, making a racket, chasing away evil spirits, and trying to frighten off winter. Traditionally, the young men hoped to use the parade as an opportunity to catch the eye of a potential wife. (What girl wouldn't want a stinky monster in green socks?) Even today, young women still toss them red handkerchiefs as a token of affection, which they proudly wrap around their necks as they carry on.

The Kurents clang their way from house to house. The woolly mob stands outside the door and makes a horrible racket, swinging their hips back and forth to rattle their bells. Eventually the homeowner relents and comes out to appease the savage beasts with food and drink. He hangs a sausage on the end of the Kurent chief's hedgehog-covered stick. His partners swing their hips loudly with satisfaction. Then the homeowner brings out strong drinks to keep the Kurent mob well-fueled. Everyone removes their headpieces just long enough to eat and socialize a bit. Then they're on their way to the next house.

Shaking their hips and making an ungodly noise, the woolly mob invades the village.

"Uglies," "Ploughmen," and More

Although guys in Kurent costumes are the most popular, there are other costumes and similar rituals in villages throughout Slovenia. Each town has its own traditional band of raucous characters in outrageous getups who rampage through the town, scaring off winter, welcoming spring, and going house to house for a gift of food and drink.

Some villages have a motley crew known only as "the uglies"—dressed in animal skins, devil masks, and horns. Another band is more joyful, dressed in tall rainbow-colored hats and prancing around a flower-draped wagon (perhaps representing spring). There's a cast of stock village characters. A "peasant woman" (a dude in drag) trundles from house to house asking for food. A group of "ploughmen" ask the farmer for permission to plow his land. They hitch the fake plow (a wagon) to some men dressed as horses, who pull it around and ceremonially unearth a big turnip, which "wakes the soil" to bring bountiful crops. Then the homeowner brings out eggs and sausage and wishes the merry band good health as all look forward to a good harvest.

What does it all mean? The traditions are so baked into village life that even the locals can only speculate. Kurentovanje dates back at least to medieval times, and probably traces back to earlier pagan traditions. Perhaps the homeowners sharing food is a remnant of the distant past when winter was hard, and families shared what they had to make it through until spring. They had to celebrate and

In colorful and scary masks, the Kurents make merry in lean times, stoking the spirit of hardscrabble peasants to get through the winter.

The woolly Kurent king, like a Slovenian Bacchus, is a fun-loving and pagan Slavic god of hedonism.

make merry even in lean times to give each other encouragement to carry on. The scary masks and costumes gave them the courage to attack the demons of winter.

(Now can someone please explain the symbolism of that hedgehog-on-a-stick?)

Dreznica—Digging Deep in Tradition

Some of Slovenia's purest traditions are found in Dreznica—an isolated mountain village far, far off the tourist path, with a population of only a few hundred. The customs here are similar to those of other Slovenian towns—frightful costumes and noise to drive off winter, pretty costumes to welcome spring, and lots of door-to-door conviviality. But there's something more going on here. It's a rite of passage for young men, ushering them into the grownup world of village life.

The Kurent ritual is a rite of passage for young boys. Bridging childhood and adulthood, they become full members of their community.

The whole affair is run by a secret club of young men, aged from around 12 to 25—a pack of tweens, teens, and young bachelors. These youngsters are making the awkward transition from childhood to adulthood. The Easter traditions help guide them along the path and bind the isolated community together.

The celebration begins in total darkness. At the stroke of midnight, all the village lights go out. The young men gather outside of town and begin a ritual tinged with classic pagan elements. They light a low-smoldering bonfire of evergreens that produces more smoke than light. Carrying torches, they sing a romantic song about the moon. Then they parade through the village, clanging and banging and shouting, waking everyone up. The Carnival party is ready to begin!

As dawn breaks, the next phase begins. The young men don costumes and are transformed into a timeless cast of characters. It's a Bizarro World mirror

Horned and smelly, the Kurents search for small boys. Finding one, they chase him down, pelt him with globs of ash, and suddenly he's part of their woolly brotherhood.

image of their own village—there's the town mayor, the doctor, the corrupt cop, the jack-of-all-trades repairman, and the housewives. Each boy chooses his costume and what role he'll play in this parallel-universe village. Thrown into the mix are some crazy symbolic characters rooted in the pagan world—a horned devil (symbolizing winter's sting), the lottery man (symbolizing how "life is like a lottery—some win, some lose"), and rainbow-dreadlocked guys who welcome the beauty of spring.

Once in costume (and in character), the young men make another parade through town. As in other Slovenian villages, they go house to house. There's lots of laughter, drinking, polka music, and gifts of food.

Then it's time to select new members for their secret brotherhood. Back in the streets, the chase is on. The devils and "uglies" hunt down the town's 12-year-old boys. The bungling "cop" tries to keep order, but it's no use. They corner the boys and—whack!—they're pelted and covered with messy bombs of dust and ash. Welcome to the club! The boys dream of the day next year when, as part of this brotherhood, they'll assume a grown-up role and become chasers themselves.

Ptuj—Slovenia's Carnival Capital

Slovenia's Carnival season culminates just before Lent in the undisputed Carnival capital—the town of Ptuj. (How to pronounce it? Just spit it out. *P-TOO-ee!*) Carnival bands from all over Slovenia converge here to strut their stuff. Visitors crowd the town for a chance to see a smorgasbord of traditions. In Ptuj's parade, everyone gets into the spirit—men, women, and children. Nowadays you can even buy a Kurent costume off the rack and join in. The Kurentovantje celebration in Ptuj lasts several days and consists of parades, masked balls, concerts, kids' events, bar-hopping, and general debauchery. The town even has a Kurentovantje museum.

The main event is the big parade on the Sunday before Ash Wednesday. Thousands of spectators line the route. Costumed revelers converge in a perfect storm

In Ptuj's parade, the entire town gets into the Carnival spirit.

of raucousness to dance along the main street. There are even clubs from other countries, brought here in a kind of "creature exchange" program.

Crack!—the parade begins. Guys slinging long (dangerous!) bullwhips snap the crowd to attention. Then those ploughmen arrive, to "wake up the soil." There's a parade of symbolic animals: giant hens (who lay the fertile eggs of Easter), high-spirited horses (representing healthy livestock), and trained bears (men in costume) herded by Gypsy women (more men in costume). An old woman carries an old man on her back, symbolizing how the memory of our departed ancestors is with us always. A horse-drawn wagon holds oranges, which are tossed to the crowd—a reminder that the bounty of warmer weather is just around the corner.

But the stars are always the Kurents. Imagine some three hundred hairy beasts, each one with five huge bells clanging at top volume, stomping down the main

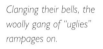

Clanging their bells, the woolly gang of "uglies" rampages on.

street while the crowd snaps photos and cheers them on. Kurent dads stop to help their Kurent kids adjust their masks. Kurent teenagers attack the crowd to sweep up pretty girls in a woolly embrace to usher in spring. Slovenia's Carnival is beamed across Europe on live TV, keeping those ancient traditions alive in the 21st century.

LENT

LENT—WILL WINTER NEVER END?

AFTER THE LAST Carnival partygoer is sent home to sleep it off, a 40-day period of sobriety begins, called Lent. It's a time of fasting and reflection as Christendom prepares for Easter.

The somber season probably has historical roots that predate Christianity. The word "Lent" means "spring" (from the Anglo-Saxon *lencten*), but in reality—it was still winter. The forced gaiety of Carnival was a false spring, and Lent was when the hard truth really set in. The foods you stored last fall were running low. The last of the meat was finished during Carnival. There would be no eggs until spring. And the barren fields were still weeks away from being ready for planting. Simply surviving the next few weeks would be a challenge. This was a time that required a strong faith. People naturally turned once again to the heavens, praying to God or the gods for aid and comfort.

ASH WEDNESDAY

After Fat Tuesday comes Ash Wednesday. The party's over.

Hungover revelers go to church for a solemn service. Worshippers shuffle up the aisle to the altar and kneel. There, the priest or pastor puts a cross of ash or dust on their forehead, which literally marks the beginning of Lent.

The ash symbolizes remorse, repentance, and ultimate purification. The Bible is full of references to ashes and dust. Ash suggests the frailty of human existence—"for dust you are and to dust you will return" (Genesis 3:19). People put ashes or dust on their heads as a sign of repentance (2 Samuel 13:19). For Job, it was a sign of humble self-examination, when he realized how little he understood of God's great plan: "Surely I spoke of things I did not understand, things too wonderful for me to know. Therefore I despise myself and repent in dust and ashes" (Job 42).

But ultimately, ash symbolizes a purifying process. In Biblical times, sacrificial

The party's over. A little ash on the forehead symbolizes repentance and purification.

offerings to God burned down to ash, thus purifying the offering by fire. In turn, the ash was used to purify the unclean. If a pastor puts the mark of ash on your forehead, it's a sign of hope—if you're truly repentant, you will be purified.

40 Days and 40 Nights

Lent lasts 40 days—from Ash Wednesday to Easter Sunday. But in fact, the exact number varies between various liturgical calendars—Catholic, Protestant, or Orthodox. Traditionally, it's called "40 days" to remember the 40 days Jesus spent in the wilderness, tempted by Satan, before beginning his ministry (Matthew 4, Mark 1, Luke 4).

Sandro Botticelli, The Temptations of Christ, 1480-82

Lent is a time of penitence and sorrow—of reflecting on Christ's suffering and our own sins. People go to church, pray, and give alms. They purify themselves through fasting, giving up a favorite activity, or other acts of self-denial. Putting aside the material distractions of the world helps them focus on what's important—God.

During Lent, many people give up certain foods. In past centuries, there were strict rules for what foods were forbidden. One document from medieval times specified that you could not eat meat, eggs, butter, or milk . . . but you could eat beaver tails.

As people purged their cupboards of forbidden foods, another tradition was born. The day before Lent—Shrove Tuesday—is observed by eating pancakes. (Brits call it Pancake Day.) It's a feast of the milk, butter, and eggs that would go bad during Lent.

Over the years, the severity of the fasting and penitence has softened, and is now mainly a personal choice. Most Europeans, unless they're especially religious, don't give Lent's dietary restrictions much thought. It may be as simple as skipping a few meals or eating lighter. You might give up a favorite food, such as chocolate, or a favorite activity, like going to the movies or texting. Catholics might skip meat

The Temptation of Christ—Matthew 4:1-17

Lent marks the time when Jesus went into the wilderness and fasted for 40 days and 40 nights. He was hungry. Satan came to him and said, "If you are the Son of God, tell these stones to become bread." Jesus answered, "Man shall not live by bread alone, but on every word that comes from the mouth of God. Away from me, Satan!" From that time on Jesus began to preach, saying: "Repent, for the Kingdom of Heaven is near."

on Fridays, and eat fish instead. Or you can observe Lent less by self-denial and more by giving to the less fortunate.

Church services during Lent are somber, anticipating the upcoming Cruci-fixion of Christ. The church might be decorated with the so-called Stations of the Cross—a series of paintings, statues, or tableaus depicting the traditional 14 stops Jesus made as he carried the cross on the road to his death and burial. The pastor might wear purple, a long-standing symbol of humility and suffering that foreshadows the royal purple robes placed on Jesus when he was mocked as "King of the Jews."

The Lenten liturgy (the prescribed worship service of Bible readings, hymns, and rituals) focuses on death, repentance, and on the frailty of man. Happy hymns sung the rest of the year are left out during Lent. You won't hear the word "Alleluia" (or Hallelujah, Praise God) because it's too joyful. "Gloria in Excelsis

Lent is a time of fasting, penitence, and reflection.

Deo" (Glory to God in the Highest) also gets deleted from the playlist, because it's how the angels rejoiced when Christ was born. Bible readings are severe: "Blow the trumpet and sound the alarm, for the day of the Lord is coming—a day of darkness and gloom, clouds and blackness" (Joel 2:1-2).

LENT RELENTS

It's not all bleak. Along the way, there are occasional glimpses of the coming joy of spring and Easter. Sundays are generally exempt from fasting. And on the fourth Sunday of Lent, roughly the midway point, the liturgy begins: "Rejoice." The minister wears festive white (rather than Lenten purple) and the scripture reading is of Jesus feeding 5,000 hungry people. Another day on the liturgical calendar is also reason to celebrate: Annunciation Day remembers the joyous event when the angel announced Jesus' impending birth to Mary. It's celebrated on March 25th—that is, nine months before Jesus' birth at Christmas.

In the UK, the fourth Sunday is "Mothering Day," the equivalent of our Mother's Day. British sons and daughters join their mums for tea time. They feast on simnel cake, a spiced fruitcake topped with 11 marzipan balls representing the apostles (sans Judas).

In fact, throughout Lent (especially on Sundays), even the most religious individuals spice up their lives with a little indulgence here and there. In Scandinavian countries, they enjoy semla, a spiced bun filled with whipped cream. It's a culinary reminder of better days to come. Then it's back to the somber treadmill.

Week by week, Lent drags along, as the world ever so slowly awakens from the drudgery of winter. The slow procession to Easter accelerates dramatically with the arrival of Holy Week.

PALM SUNDAY

HOLY WEEK BEGINS

HOLY WEEK, the week leading up to Easter Sunday, is the most sacred time of the Christian year. It's the week when Jesus arrived in Jerusalem, celebrated a Last Supper with his followers, and was arrested, tried, tortured, and executed. Each day, the faithful recount the various events from the Bible.

The week is an emotional and spiritual roller coaster. It goes from the excitement of Jesus' arrival to the agony of his death, the gloom of his burial, and finally the joyous morning of his Resurrection on Easter Sunday. Christians call this series of events "the Passion," for the suffering of Jesus (from the Latin *pati*).

The Bible makes it clear that the events of Holy Week took place during the Jewish holiday of Passover. Remember, Jesus was a Jew who ate a Passover meal with his disciples (the Last Supper) to commemorate the ancient Israelites' exo-

Holy Week begins with Palm Sunday, as the faithful take to the streets with palm fronds, recalling Jesus' triumphal entry into Jerusalem.

In Greece, children know that a little quality time with godparents comes with a tasty Easter treat.

dus from slavery in Egypt. Even today, the word for "Easter" in many European countries derives from the Hebrew word for Passover, *Pesah*. Greeks call Easter *Pascha*, Italians say *Pasqua*, it's *Pâques* in French, and *Pascuas* in Spain. Though Christian Holy Week and Jewish Passover are forever linked in history, they're now celebrated at different times. That's because the date of Easter is arrived at by convention (see page 30) and is no longer tied to the Jewish calendar.

For children, Holy Week is a cause for celebration—this is when the excitement of Easter really ramps up. Chocolate bunnies appear in store windows. Families decorate their homes with chicks and daffodils and school art projects and plastic grass. Kids get to dye Easter eggs. Invitations are sent for Easter dinner, there are shopping trips to the markets, and homes are filled with the aroma of cinnamon and fresh-baked goods.

Holy Week in Europe offers a full eight days of events. The celebrations range from the depths of spiritual sorrow (remembering Jesus' Passion) to the hope of spring, from the warmth of friends and family to the screaming excitement of little kids on a sugary Easter high.

Let's take the week day by day. We'll see how all across Europe—from Spain to Slovenia, Britain to Germany, Italy to Greece—there are different traditions, some similar to America's and some very different. We'll also see how each culture puts a different emphasis on a different day of the week.

It all starts one week before Easter, on Palm Sunday.

PALMS, POPES, AND PARADES

Palm Sunday was the day when Jesus entered Jerusalem to a hero's welcome by his followers. Jesus rode in on a donkey (fulfilling an ancient prophecy), while his followers shouted "Hosanna! Blessings on him who comes in the name of the

With High Church spectacle, the pope kicks off Holy Week each Palm Sunday in front of St. Peter's Basilica.

The faithful gather early in hopes of snaring a good perch from which to see the pope.

Lord!" It's called "Palm" Sunday because the followers laid down branches before him (though the Bible does not specify what tree they came from). The reception Jesus received followed the custom of the day, when Romans welcomed royalty and conquering heroes with their version of a ticker-tape parade.

Europe's grandest Palm Sunday parade takes place at ground zero of European Christendom—St. Peter's Basilica at the Vatican, in the city of Rome. It was here that, 2,000 years ago, the Apostle Peter—Jesus' chief disciple and the man who brought the Christian faith to Europe—was killed and buried. The obelisk in front of the church is the same one that marked the ancient Roman chariot race course where Peter was crucified and buried. St. Peter's church was built atop his tomb. Ever since, Peter's successors as Bishop of Rome have called themselves by the title of "pope." Today, Earth's 1.2 billion Catholics recognize the pope as their spiritual leader and St. Peter's as their spiritual center.

Early in the morning of Palm Sunday, tens of thousands of faithful Catholics converge on the 300,000-foot expanse of St. Peter's Square. Many stand for hours, packing the oval-shaped piazza. Forests of palm fronds are a reminder of Jesus' triumphant entry, and people enthusiastically wave palm branches. You can feel the energy. There are people from all over the world—Nigerian nuns, Mexican theology students, accountants from Ohio. For many of the faithful, this is the ultimate pilgrimage—to be at the source of their faith on Palm Sunday.

Around 10:00 a.m., the beautifully orchestrated event officially begins. A parade of priests in white enters the square, carrying palms, olive branches, and crosses. They're followed by other frond-bearing priests, cardinals, bishops, and plenty of dark-suited security guards. Then the pope, dressed in bright red vestments and carrying a staff, arrives and slowly makes his way to the podium. He addresses the crowd and blesses the palms (and a few babies). Then he says a

Mass. The magnificent backdrop for this ceremony is St. Peter's Basilica, topped with Michelangelo's soaring dome.

These days, Palm Sunday is celebrated all over Europe, in churches both grand and humble, by worshippers singing and praying. They carry branches, fronds, or sprigs of either palm or olive. Both species are evergreen, symbolic of the promise of everlasting life. It's a tradition in some places to twist the palms into elaborate designs, crosses, or garlands. The branches for little kids might have sweets or tinsel attached.

During the service, parishioners have their branches blessed. Many churches draw some of their biggest crowds of the year, so they might use the occasion to give First Communion to the congregation's youngsters. The service concludes with the minister blessing the bread and wine for Communion. This ritual ceremonially recreates the sacrament of Communion instituted by Jesus at the Last Supper, 2,000 years ago.

In churches grand and humble throughout Italy, parishioners bring olive branches (more readily available than palm fronds) to be blessed.

HOLY MONDAY

Spain's Semana Santa

While Rome kicks off Holy Week with a grand Palm Sunday spectacle, the festivities continue with special fervor in Spain. Here, Holy Week is known as Semana Santa, a time of pageantry and time-worn tradition. Each day of the week features a different parade as the emotion builds towards Easter.

Spain—separated from the rest of Europe by the Pyrenees Mountains—has developed a unique identity and heritage, and this is reflected in their Easter traditions. This country that's produced so many saints, mystics, heretics, and the Spanish Inquisition really knows how to bring passion to the Passion.

Spain's Holy Week rites are centuries old—some date back to medieval times.

Holy Week is celebrated with gusto in Spain, especially in Sevilla and the southern region of Andalucía.

The best-known events are the parades. These feature penitents dressed in eerie medieval-looking robes, walking through the streets. The hooded penitents accompany wooden floats decorated with statues depicting the events of Jesus' last days. These processions can be marathon affairs, lasting for hours on end. Some are at night, with the participants bearing torches or tall candles, or with statues lit by elaborate electric chandeliers.

The most famous Semana Santa takes place in Sevilla, southern Spain's leading city. It's the birthplace of several of the country's trademarks—bullfighting, flamenco, the Inquisition. Sevilla's parading tradition dates back to 1604. Holy Week is an epic event that stirs the soul and captivates all who participate.

Sevilla's Holy Week kicks off on Palm Sunday. Families dress up and head to their parish church for Mass. Then, promenading with palm and olive branches, they make a loop through the neighborhood, eventually returning to their church.

The first parade of floats begins. Appropriately for Palm Sunday, the star is a float with the beloved statue nicknamed La Borriquita—the Little Donkey. The donkey is carrying a statue of Jesus into Jerusalem, accompanied by happy statues waving palm branches. When La Borriquita leaves its home church and begins making its way through the narrow streets, everyone knows Holy Week is officially underway. From now on, every day until Easter Sunday, the city is enlivened with dozens of such processions.

During Holy Week, beloved statues are taken down from their altars to be paraded through the streets.

Adoring the Floats

Sevilla has more than a hundred different floats, or *pasos*. They're decorated with colorful painted wooden statues. For Holy Week, some statues are outfitted with actual cloth robes to complete the illusion. These tableaus of Bible scenes present the Passion in a way the average person can understand. Parents use the statues to talk to their kids about religious matters, as well as how to deal with complex emotions like suffering and grief.

For most of the year, the statues reside in their parish church, atop the altar. For Holy Week, they're brought down to ground level, in preparation for being mounted on the float. During that brief window of time, people are allowed to visit the churches for a chance to view the statues close up. On Monday of Holy Week, literally thousands of Sevillanos line up for hours to see one of the most impressive statues, known as Jesus del Gran Poder—Jesus of the Great Power. This evocative statue shows a bowed Jesus with a Crown of Thorns, lugging his heavy cross. It's not paraded until Good Friday, so this is their chance for an intimate encounter. Up close, they can witness Jesus, exhausted from his humiliation and beating at the hands of his captors, taking up the cross—symbolic of the burdens we all must carry. Many kiss the hand of El Gran Poder. Many weep.

In churches all across town there are similar rituals—people waiting in line to kiss the foot of Jesus, or the hand of Mary.

Dozens of Virgins—¿Quién es mas bonita?

Sevillanos hold a special place in their hearts for the floats depicting the Virgin Mary, the mother of Christ. Many Catholics routinely pray to Mary, seeing her as a sympathetic ear who will intercede for them in their troubles. During Holy Week, people get a once-a-year opportunity to interact with the Virgin face-to-face—convinced she will empathize with their needs and hear their prayers.

Mary knows the sorrow of ordinary mortals, because she had to experience the unspeakable sorrow of watching her son die.

There are dozens of statues of the Virgin Mary in Sevilla's churches. Each one evokes a different aspect of her complex emotions. The Mary known as La Estrella (for the star-like halo that frames her head) has jewel-like tears streaming down her face and a mouth contorted in grief. She has just lost her son. Embedded in her namesake star is a supposed piece of the actual cross on which Jesus was crucified.

The Mary known as La Macarena is as precious as a 17th-century doll. This statue comes complete with actual human hair, articulated arms, and an elaborate cloth dress. Her beautiful expression is halfway between smiling and crying. She's the favorite of Spain's bullfighters who consider her their protector. She smiles for them when they win and cries for them when they're injured.

The Mary known as Soledad, or solitude, rides atop the final float of Semana Santa, reminding everyone of her great loneliness after her son was gone.

Catholics have a special place in
their hearts for Mary. Just as Mary
empathizes with them, they empathize
with her sorrow over her great loss.

In Sevilla, it seems everyone is caught up in preparations for Holy Week festivities.

If Easter is mainly about Christ's suffering and death, these Mary statues allow us to see that suffering from an acutely poignant perspective—through the eyes of a grieving mother. In Sevilla, it's not just the Passion of Christ, but the Passion of Mary.

SEVILLA PREPARES

The excitement builds as people make the preparations for their upcoming parade. The task of decorating the statues and parading the floats falls to brotherhoods who donate their time. Each of Sevilla's 60 or so neighborhoods (with their neighborhood churches) has one of these religious organizations consisting of men, women, and even young children. Besides their Semana Santa duties, these venerable organizations are all involved in charitable works—funding foreign missions or social causes like helping the poor.

People decorate the floats lovingly. The float itself is a sturdy wooden frame used year after year. They cover it with a decorated cloth, and adorn it with flowers and rows and rows of tall candles. Huge silver candlesticks are polished until they gleam. Hundreds of flower petals have to be plucked. These are used for showering upon their statue of Mary when she takes her turn parading through the city. Finally, the statues are moved from public display, mounted atop the float, and arranged to create a realistic scene. With all the decorations, the whole float can weigh up to 5,000 pounds. Great care is taken to make sure that the floats are perfect in every way.

In the streets, the city of Sevilla prepares. Along the parade route, they construct temporary ramps to cover any stairsteps that might cause the float-bearers

to stumble. Chairs and grandstands are readied for the lucky few who'll get to sit (because they paid for the privilege). Hundreds of heavy crosses are laid along the route, ready to be picked up by penitents and paraded through town. Incense that perfumes the air all week is sold on the street. Prime viewing balconies along the parade route are elaborately draped with red velvet or specially-embroidered shawls. If you happen to be fortunate enough to have such a balcony, you're suddenly very popular, and you invite all your friends.

Bakeries start cranking out special Semana Santa treats. There are sweet cookies and *pestiños*—deep-fried slabs of dough dusted with sugar. Another popular Lent/Holy Week treat is *torrijas*. These are bread slices soaked in milk, battered with egg, fried up, and sweetened—sort of a Spanish French toast.

Sevillanos make sure their parade costumes are ready. Tailoring shops are buzzing with customers getting last-minute fittings. Some of the shops have been producing costumes for 200 years, and much of the work is still stitched by hand.

The city's intensive preparations sound like a lot of work, but there's much joy—people pause to refuel by popping into the tapas bars. They enjoy (meatless) pre-Easter plates like salt cod fritters, and break into spontaneous Easter time songs. In homes all across the city, people get ready for their church's

For the big Semana Santa parades, VIPs get chairs and balconies.

parade. Parents help their kids don costumes, encouraging their participation in this sacred centuries-old Easter ritual. Sevilla even sets Wednesday aside for a children's parade.

THE PARADES

Each day brings another set of parades. Think of it. These parades are what the brotherhoods have been preparing for all year long. Finally, their turn has come. They gather at their home church and get into their costumes. They pick up their float, and start heading for Sevilla's cathedral.

It's a spectacle. Many are dressed in robes. They're penitents (or *nazarenos*), bemoaning their sins. The most distinct feature of their getup is hard to miss—they wear pointed, cone-shaped hats, covered with a hood. Unfortunately, for

TOP *Reenacting scenes from the original Holy Week, elaborate floats parade for hours through the city streets, jammed with people caught up in the excitement.*

BOTTOM *Traditional robes and cones (which predate KKK garb by centuries) show how all sinners are equally deserving of forgiveness in the eyes of God.*

most Americans, these masked figures evoke the (gulp) Ku Klux Klan. But these outfits predate the racist KKK by centuries. The original purpose of the hoods was to hide the face, so that sinners could repent in anonymity.

The penitents accompany the floats through narrow alleyways as they slowly make their way to the cathedral (then eventually back to their home church). The journey, through miles of passionate crowds, can take up to 12 hours. Strong men called *costaleros* work in shifts, carrying the floats on their shoulders or the backs of their necks. (They do use a cushion.) As a team, they bear two tons of weight. They consider the experience a great honor—not despite but because of the pain involved. They know it's easier than carrying a cross.

Spectators are visibly moved. Some wipe away tears as they ponder Christ's suffering and sacrifice. Others relive memories of their childhoods, when they witnessed these same scenes with their parents. Flamenco singers in the crowd,

Strong men called costaleros *wait their turn to carry a float.*

overcome with emotion, break into timeless, mournful songs (called *saetas*), as the sad statues of Jesus or weeping Mary pass by.

Holy Week's processions peak on Good Friday, with the longest and most passionate parade. It starts Thursday evening and continues all night long until dawn. Drumming bands set a somber beat. Penitents trudge along carrying candles. Clouds of incense add an air of sweet mystery. The statues, borne atop the shoulders of sweating men, sway back and forth through the crowds, bringing the tableaus to life. Mary appears, ethereal and radiant, lit by hundreds of candles. A shower of petals rains down on her, as if heaven itself is thanking her for her immense and loving sacrifice.

TUESDAY AND WEDNESDAY

Building Up to Easter

Across Europe, families prepare for Easter, enjoying the secular traditions of the holiday, such as baking special treats and decorating Easter eggs.

Meanwhile, as Holy Week unfolds, the Passion story heats up. According to the Bible, after Jesus' entrance into Jerusalem on Palm Sunday, he begins to antagonize the Jewish authorities: He angrily drives corrupt salesmen out of the temple. He speaks ominously about the end times. When the priests try to pin him down on whether he's the promised messiah who will lead the Jewish nation to freedom, Jesus talks in mysterious parables.

Jesus is growing more and more popular with the people. The Jewish authorities are afraid that he will spark a rebellion, and that their Roman overlords will

Much of the Easter tradition is edible—tasty and full of symbolism.

Eggs represented birth and fertility long before Easter.

come down hard on the entire Jewish nation. So they secretly plot to get rid of Jesus. They hire Judas, one of Jesus' 12 disciples, to turn Jesus over to them. The plot thickens, as Jesus and his disciples prepare to gather on Holy Thursday for Passover dinner.

Devout Christians mark each day of Holy Week with church services that remember Jesus' struggles. But everyone also knows that Easter ultimately has a happy ending—Jesus' Resurrection. So Holy Week is also a time of joyous anticipation, a time to prepare for the happy occasion ahead. There's shopping to do, gifts to buy, and special foods to prepare. It's the time to dye eggs, decorate the house, and get your Easter outfit dry-cleaned. Families and friends make plans to get together.

In this chapter, we'll take a look at some of these traditions—both religious and secular—from around Europe. At Easter, solemn religious rituals and secular hijinks are woven together. Some customs are very old; some are more recent and commercialized. Europeans today celebrate some of the same secular traditions familiar to Americans—egg-decorating, gift-giving, candy, and even the Easter Bunny.

As Holy Week builds to Easter Sunday, every country and every family has its own individual set of traditions to celebrate the season. From magical creatures to chocolate eggs to grandma's special pastry, Europe has it all. Here's a sampling.

EASTER EGGS—DYEING AND REBIRTH

Eggs have been associated with the Easter season since earliest times. In the Pre-Christian world, eggs (from which new life springs) naturally symbolized birth and fertility. The ancient Romans thought of them as microcosms of the universe. They believed the cosmos came to life like a chick cracking through the shell. For the Germanic people who worshipped Eostre (the goddess of spring with her egg-laying hare), eggs symbolized rebirth, like what happens to the Earth every spring. After dying in winter, the world is reborn when fields green up again, and nature is in bloom.

It's easy to see how, as Christianity co-opted earlier traditions, the egg came to be associated with the Resurrection. The imagery dovetailed perfectly—Christ's tomb was like an egg that cracked open, and he emerged again full of life.

Elaborately decorated eggs symbolize and celebrate rebirth and the Resurrection.

Eggs took on an added significance in medieval times. Back then, eggs (being animal products) were often forbidden for those 40 days of Lent. Consequently, people went egg-crazy once the controlled substance was finally legalized, gorging on eggs for the Easter meal (as people still do today). In their anticipation, people collected eggs in the days leading up to Easter. They dyed and painted these treasured items, displayed them prominently in their homes, and gave them to friends as gifts.

Egg decorating has become an art form. In Russia in the late 19th century, Carl Fabergé began making Easter "eggs" for the Tsars, decorated with elaborate metal work and studded with jewels. These are now displayed in museums around the world. In Greece, people decorate ostrich eggs, which they display in their churches, dangling from ornate chandeliers.

Around 1900, an American named William Townley brought egg-dyeing to the masses. He put the dye in tablet form. Plunk! You just dissolved it in a little water and vinegar. Townley branded his invention Paas, after a Dutch word for Easter. Now even little kids can create beautiful eggs, and egg-decorating has become a family tradition in even the busiest modern households.

EGGS ACROSS EUROPE

Today, eggs continue to be a recurring Easter theme throughout Europe. Every country (and family) has their own different tradition.

When it comes to dyeing eggs, some start with eggs that are hard-boiled. Others use hollowed-out eggs: You poke holes with a needle on either end of the raw egg, then blow through one of the holes to force the yolk out the other end. Some Europeans decorate the egg using traditional methods—hand-painting with natural pigments. But more and more, people these days just dunk the eggs in commercial dyes (like Paas) or simple food coloring.

In Germanic lands, the fun doesn't stop there. After dyeing the (hollowed-out)

Greeks dye their eggs red to symbolize the blood Christ shed on the cross.

eggs, people use them for decorations. They might put a string on the ends of the eggs and hang them outside from trees and bushes—like Christmas ornaments. Or they might hang the eggs from a little indoor Easter tree—either real or artificial. Others display their eggs in a wicker Easter basket with fake grass, or among sprigs of daffodils or pussy willows.

Once decorated and placed out for display, the Easter eggs sit as a reminder to all of the upcoming joy of Easter Sunday.

TRADITIONAL EGG DYEING IN SLOVENIA

One place where eggs are still decorated the old-fashioned way is the remote region of Bela Krajina, in Slovenia. Here, in villages tucked among the hills and forests, is where many of Slovenia's folk tales were born and old customs live on.

These dyeing techniques date back to medieval times. The dyes are natural—from wine, beetroot, nettles, onion skins, and so on. In one technique, fresh spring leaves and flowers are gathered and pressed onto the egg. The whole thing is wrapped tightly in gauze and placed in a natural dye. After the shell is colored and the gauze removed, the eggs are left with an imprint of the flowers and leaves—stamps of springtime.

In another technique, they draw a pattern onto the shell with a tool loaded with hot beeswax. They then dye the egg with natural colors. The part where there's wax remains undyed. (American kids use a similar technique with a wax crayon.) After the dye dries, you can draw on the egg again, and dip it into another color, and so on. The result is an elaborately-patterned egg of several colors. The most traditional patterns are geometric—zigzags, crosses, spirals. There are also floral

The medieval Slovenian egg-dyeing tradition survives today. The exquisitely decorated eggs are not only treasured gifts but are also preserved in museums.

designs, and even writing names or personal messages to loved ones. The final step is to finish the egg by rubbing it in pig's fat to lend a nice sheen. Eggs decorated in the traditional way by local masters are recognized as folk art, and their work is displayed in Slovenian museums.

Slovenes are proud of this heritage. Kids learn the age-old techniques, and even the least-artistic take a stab at it. Giving a hand-decorated egg to someone as an Easter gift is a big deal. Slovenes today say these eggs are not expensive—they're priceless.

SURPRISE! THE ITALIAN CHOCOLATE EGG

Italians also have a tradition of giving eggs at Easter—chocolate ones.

As Easter approaches, shop windows from Rome to Florence to Milan are filled with colorful displays of chocolate Easter eggs wrapped in colorful foil or cellophane. Some are big and expensive, some small and cheap. Some are meant only for eating. Others are huge, hollow, and come with a surprise inside.

Giving someone a chocolate egg with a surprise gift inside has become a playful Easter tradition in recent years. You don't know what's inside until you bite in. Most commercial brands come with simple Cracker-Jack-style trinkets—a little toy or key chain. At the very low end is a kids' brand called Kinder Eggs—invented by an Italian company, and now a pop-culture staple everywhere in Europe.

At the high end, some specialty shops hand-make top-quality artisanal chocolate eggs, and work with the customer to put a custom gift inside.

To make an Italian hollow chocolate egg: Melt chocolate and pour onto a flat surface. Smooth with a spatula until there are no air bubbles. Pour the still-hot chocolate into two molds—the two halves of an egg. As you pour, turn the molds (here's where you need an experienced hand) to spread the chocolate evenly. When cool, remove the two half-eggs. Place your surprise inside, maybe with some fake grass to hold it in place. Put the two halves together, fusing the seam

Italians reaffirm their love for each other by hiding a gift—perhaps a necklace—in a chocolate egg. And the pastry chef knows just how to make it all possible.

by painting it with melted chocolate. Wrap it in cellophane and tie it with a bow, and—*Ecco!*—a Chocolate Surprise Egg.

With some advance planning and some help from behind the counter, you can arrange to hide a special gift inside. For a child, it might be a little toy. For a friend, maybe two concert tickets. Husbands give necklaces or earrings to their wives as an affirmation of their love. And some lucky ladies have broken one open, found a ring inside, and are suddenly met with the exciting question— "Will you marry me?"

EASTER BUNNY—WHICH CAME FIRST, THE BUNNY OR THE EGG?

The biggest gift-giver of all is that hirsute, plantigrade, phantasmagorical leporid known as the Easter Bunny.

There's some version of the Easter Bunny in the traditions of many European cultures. As mentioned earlier (see page 24), legends may date as far back as the pagan goddess Eostre and her mammalian sidekick who could lay eggs. Rabbits and hares (which are notoriously prolific breeders) have been a symbol of new life since earliest times.

Germany is the chief source of many well-known Easter legends—just like it gave us popular Christmas legends like Santa Claus.

In ancient times, the Germanic regions remained outside the sphere of the Roman Empire and early Christianity. They stayed "barbarian" and pagan well into medieval times. The name of one of the Germanic goddesses, Eostre (or Ostara), may be the source of the German word for Easter—*Ostern*. (And the German name *Ostern* is where we get our English word "Easter.") Remember that most European countries derive their name for Easter from the Christian word for Passover (e.g., *Pasqua*), but Germany's name shows the region's pagan roots.

Tales of Eostre's egg-laying rabbit continued to breed prolifically through the Middle Ages. The legends first entered the historical record in the 16th century, in German documents that mentioned that the rabbit or hare was a symbol of Easter. Since then, the legend has grown. Parents would tell their kids that if they were good, a bunny would bring them candy.

It was also in Germany that we see the first edible Easter Bunnies, made of pastry and sugar, produced in the early 1800s. Also, German children made nests of grass and—on the night before Easter Sunday—they set them in the garden for the Easter Bunny to fill during the night with brightly decorated eggs.

These German traditions made their way to America with Pennsylvania Dutch immigrants. In America, children made nests out of their hats and bonnets for the Easter Bunny to come and fill.

Even today in Germany, the Easter Bunny lives on. He's called the *Osterhase*—literally "Easter Hare." German kids still dye eggs. They still build an Easter nest for the bunny to fill—gathering moss and leaves from the yard (or using plastic grass). *Grossmutter* (grandma) might even bake a special cake in the form of a bunny to place in the nest. And on Easter Sunday morning, the lucky kids wake to find their nest filled with goodies.

It's good to know that after 2,500 years of making his rounds, the Easter Bunny is still bringing it. Little German kids still grow up believing in that fecund magical creature who blesses the world with eggs, candy, and joy.

OTHER MAGICAL GIFT-GIVING CREATURES

Though not every European culture has an Easter Bunny per se, most have some kind of magical gift-bringer at Easter time. In Switzerland, an Easter cuckoo bird brings the eggs. In Italy (as we've seen), it's not the bunny that brings eggs and gifts, it's your friends and family.

France has Easter fish and Easter bells. The Flying Bells (*Cloche Volant*) are depicted as just that—church bells with a pair of wings. According to legend, they fly to Rome on Good Friday to see the pope and drop off everyone's misery over the Crucifixion. Then, relieved of grief, they return home on Easter morning, bringing joy and chocolate and eggs. Kids leave nests or baskets out overnight for the magical bells to fill.

France's Easter fish is not a gift-bearer, but an Easter gift in itself. It derives

Bunny, Rabbit, or Hare?

Neither biologists, historians, nor cultural anthropologists can agree on exactly what species the Easter Bunny is. But we do know what science says about bunnies in general:

Rabbits and hares, though morphologically related, are distinctly different species. Hares are bigger and stronger, with longer ears and longer hind legs. Rabbits are smaller and cuter (and tastier, say the French). Rabbits are social creatures, while hares are solitary. Both reproduce prolifically—bearing a litter of five to six young every two months. A baby hare is called a "leveret," so only a young rabbit can truly be called a "bunny."

from an April Fool's Day tradition, where kids stick a paper fish on the backs of adults as a practical joke, and yell *"Poisson d'Avril!"* (April fish!). It's so much fun that a fish-shaped sweet has become an Easter standard. Shops sell chocolate fish or hollow eggs filled with fish-shaped candies.

Throughout France, pastry shops are soon filled with a menagerie of Easter-related sweets: fish, bells, bunnies, chicks, eggs, and so on. French people love strolling the streets admiring the artistry of shop displays as they engage in the popular custom of window-shopping. (Or, as the phrase is rendered in French, *lèche-vitrines*—"window-licking.") Leave it to the food-loving French to make the focus of their Easter be about giving and enjoying the tastiest and best-quality chocolates and pastries, fashioned into the magical symbols of Easter.

THE COLORS OF EASTER

Traditional Easter colors are green (symbolizing spring growth) and yellow (the sun). Little wonder that green-and-yellow daffodils (which flower early) and early-blooming pussy-willows have become harbingers of the season. The Easter lily is also a symbol of Easter. It may be because Jesus talked about "the lilies of the field" or because lilies supposedly sprouted miraculously from the spilt blood of Christ. Chicks and ducklings represent Easter because they are new life hatched from eggs (and because they're cute).

These icons—religious and secular—have become big business. Florists get a flurry of orders, bakeries make treats, and grocers stock up for people shopping for special dinners.

In Prague, locals set up an Easter market in the Old Town Square. It's a great way to kick off the spring—browsing the wooden stalls, surrounded by the

Daffodils are among this holiday's top-selling flowers.

square's unbeatable ambience of colorful pastel buildings, a 250-foot tower, and the city's trademark trapezoidal turrets. Visitors can buy handmade crafts and watch villagers painting eggs the old-fashioned way. And then take a break at one of the delightful outdoor cafés to sip a fine Czech pilsner (good any time of year).

For European candy manufacturers, Easter is one of the busiest seasons of the year. In times past, sweets were a reward after the scarcity of winter and severity of Lent. With spring approaching, you knew you could gorge yourself, because more was on the way. Today, even the least-religious of Europeans still observe the season with some kind of goody basket of sweets for their kids (or themselves).

Though it's difficult in the global economy to trace which candies are distinctly "European" and which come from elsewhere, there are some trademark European

treats. British kids love their Cadbury Creme Eggs. Germany has embraced Kinder Eggs with a passion. France has its artisanal chocolate fish and Italy has the hollow eggs. And what about those marshmallow chicks and bunnies called Peeps? These distinctly American treats (invented in the States in the 1950s) have now crossed the Atlantic to the Old Country and become a seemingly unstoppable invasive species.

THE SOUNDS OF SPRING

Jingle, jangle, shake! Clack, clack, clack!

In the small towns of Britain, Holy Week heralds the arrival of the Morris dancers. Since medieval times, high-spirited men have strapped on anklets of bells and danced through the streets, chasing away winter and welcoming spring. Today, folk-dancing clubs keep the tradition alive. They generally wear white clothes, with colorful accessories—vests, sashes, breeches, stockings, or straw hats adorned with flowers. The Morris men shake their bells and an accordion player plays a tune, as they leap and kick and strut and do-si-do. They might carry scarves that they wave in unison, or carry sticks that they clack together in rhythm.

Europe has a long tradition of itinerant musicians or troubadours roving the countryside and spreading joy at springtime. In Italy, it still goes on in the small villages of the Marche region. Here, the mountains seem to cradle Easter rituals trapped in their deep valleys. Folk bands of troubadours go from farm to farm. It's the new spring, and they're here to bless the coming harvest. They rouse the

In Italy's Marche region, colorfully clad folk troubadours bring holiday cheer and a harvest blessing to remote farmsteads.

village with their music. And then, as is the tradition, they're invited to enjoy the fruits of last year's harvest—some bread, farm-made cheese, salami, and wine.

EASTER: THE GATHERING

Easter is a gathering time—for friends, families, and extended families. As Easter approaches, young professionals in big cities (where no one who lives there was actually born there) reserve their high-speed train tickets to return to their home-towns. Some part of Holy Week almost invariably is a national holiday, a school spring break, or at least a three-day weekend.

This is a time when generations come together. Mom, grandma, and the little ones put on aprons and roll up their sleeves in the kitchen. In Greece, it's a tra-dition for children to pay a visit to their godparents, who play a big role in the

Throughout Christendom, children's choirs brighten retirement homes.

Orthodox faith. The godparents might give their godchild a chocolate egg or a special candle to hold at the upcoming Resurrection ceremony on Easter Sunday.

Easter is a time when people remember those who have no families. Preschoolers visit retirement homes to bring some Easter joy with skits and songs that take the seniors back to their childhoods. And the seniors respond with gifts of their own.

EASTER FOODS

Easter everywhere is celebrated with special foods—foods imbedded in the cultural heritage as well as family favorites. Holy Week is the time to plan menus, go shopping for the big Easter Sunday meal, and bake special treats in advance. Those who rarely cook might at least tackle a few things at Easter time. Those who never cook at all still go shopping at the artisanal delis for precooked Easter favorites.

In every country and through the whole Easter season—from Lent to Easter—there's one common denominator: baked goods. Every family and every cultural tradition has its own special variation on dough, spiced with cinnamon and sugar.

Hot cross buns are especially popular. These are lightly-sweetened raisin buns with a cross on top made of icing. Traditionally (but not exclusively), they're

One a penny, two a penny: Hot cross buns are a tasty reminder of the Easter story.

eaten on Good Friday—hence, the symbolism of the cross of Jesus' Crucifixion. The English even had a Good Friday song that's been passed down to us as a nursery rhyme: "Hot cross buns, hot cross buns, one-a-penny, two-a-penny, hot cross buns."

Italian mamas specialize in *schiacciata di pasqua*, an anise-flavored Easter cake that they make only once a year. In Greece, an Easter treat is braided bread (reminiscent of Jewish challah) called *tsoureki*. And I've already mentioned *torrijas* (Spanish French toast), which gives Spaniards their superhuman parade-watching endurance.

Baked goodies are not only packed with sugar and spice—they also come loaded with symbolism. *Colomba*, an Italian fruitcake similar to *panettone*, is shaped in a mold so it comes out looking like a dove—the dove of the Holy Spirit.

Italian *ciambelli* is round, symbolizing the Crown of Thorns. In Germany, they use a mold to bake up the beloved *Osterlämmchen* (Easter lambkin) or a baked *Osterhase* (Easter hare) to go into the kids' nest of goodies.

In Slovenia, locals make an unforgettable pilgrimage to a bakery that makes another symbolic Easter

On Slovenia's scenic Lake Bled, a tiny island has a bakery and a church—each very busy on Easter.

treat. The bakery sits on an incredibly picturesque island in the center of incredibly picturesque Lake Bled, nestled at the foot of the snow-dusted Julian Alps. Slovenians from across the country board small ferry boats to reach the tiny island across the glass-like lake. The island has a small church and a tiny bakery. Here, Slovenians honor the Virgin Mary at the church and then step next door to buy some of Slovenia's famous Easter bread called *potica* (poh-TEETS-zah).

Potica is made of sweet dough rolled out flat. You cover this with a paste of honey, nuts, raisins, and cinnamon. Then you roll it up into a log. You bend the log into a circle and place it into a circular ceramic bundt pan. After it's baked, it pops out as a delicious, symbolic version of Jesus' Crown of Thorns.

Baked goods during Lent are just the warmup. As Easter Sunday approaches, the family chef starts prepping for the upcoming Sunday meal—scouring the markets for the best-quality lamb and ham, and preparing the side dishes ahead of time. Oh, and one other step. First, the foods should be blessed.

Blessing of Foods

Many church-going Europeans follow the centuries-old custom of bringing Easter foods to their minister to have them blessed in preparation for their Easter meal.

They prepare the blessing basket. In Slovenia, village women gather—just as their grandmothers did—to work together. They pack foods in a basket, as if they're going to a holy picnic. There are hard-boiled eggs, which have been carefully decorated (but will be eaten later). Links of sausage represent the ropes that bound Jesus. Traditional smoked pork represents Christ's body, which is to be sacrificed. Pointy horseradish roots are the nails on Jesus' cross. The *potica* is the Crown of Thorns. Some eggs are dyed red, for the blood Christ shed. After the women finish packing their baskets, they cover them with lovingly embroidered cloths.

They take the baskets to their church for a special Holy Week service. They dress in their best clothes. For simple Slovenian farmers, this might be just a plain white linen outfit they wove themselves. Their closest church might be as simple as a humble roadside chapel. Similar ceremonies go on in time-passed Tuscan hill towns and whitewashed Tirolean villages.

Slovenian women lovingly embroider cloths to cover baskets filled with food for lavish Easter feasts.

The village priest waves his hand over the baskets, saying a quick blessing. It's a thank-you to God for the bounty, and a way to ensure that the foods will bring good health and salvation. These blessed foods go back home to await the big moment—when they'll be enjoyed with friends and family on Easter Sunday.

And so, day by day, Holy Week moves on. The family has been invited, the breads have been baked, the eggs have been dyed, the foods have been blessed, and the chocolate eggs have been ogled. Mom's ready for a break. As Thursday approaches, it's time for the secular preparations to get a temporary rest, as the spiritual side of Holy Week kicks into high gear.

HOLY (OR "MAUNDY") THURSDAY

THE LAST SUPPER

ACCORDING TO THE BIBLE, the Thursday before Easter is when Jesus and his 12 disciples celebrated the "Feast of Unleavened Bread"—that is, the Jewish Passover. Christians know this meal as Jesus' Last Supper.

That night, as they ate the Passover meal together, Jesus introduced a new ritual that Christians everywhere have practiced ever since. Jesus broke bread and told his disciples, "This is my body." He poured wine and said it was his blood. Christians today recreate this Last Supper symbolically with a bite of bread (or wafer) and a sip of wine (or juice)—a ceremony called Communion or the Eucharist. By eating the bread and wine, Christians remember the sacrifice Christ gave of his own life so they could be forgiven and saved in the eyes of God. It's the essence of the Easter story.

During that Last Supper, Jesus also turned to his disciples and said: "Truly, one of you will betray me." They responded, "Lord, is it I?" After the meal, Jesus and his disciples went to Gethsemane. Jesus knew the horrible fate that awaited him, and he prayed to God that he be excused from it if it was possible. But right on cue, Judas showed up with a band of armed men. He greeted Jesus with a kiss—the signal to the soldiers that this was their man. There was a small skirmish. But the Bible makes it clear that ultimately "all of the disciples left him and fled." Alone, Jesus was arrested and led off to the authorities. The agony of the Passion was underway.

"MAUNDY" THURSDAY

Christians everywhere commemorate that important night's events with church services that start at sunset and might stretch until midnight. For Catholics, Holy Thursday is one of the most sacred Masses in the Catholic calendar, full of ancient ritual and mysticism.

Even in Protestant churches, it's a somber service. The church's decor—crosses, iconography, and religious artwork—are covered in purple drapery. As mentioned earlier, purple represents the humility with which Jesus would have to endure the events of the Passion.

The Holy Thursday liturgy brings out the link between the Christian Passion and the Jewish Passover. Worshippers read aloud the Bible accounts (Exodus 12) of how Moses freed his Israelites from bondage and led them on the Exodus from Egypt (which historians speculate may have happened around 1200 B.C.). On the night of Passover, Moses commanded his people to slaughter a lamb and mark their doors with the lamb's blood so that God's vengeance against the Egyptians would "pass over" their households and spare them. Then they ate the lamb to fuel up for their escape. Jews today remember this night with a ritual meal called the Seder.

For Christians, the symbolism of the Passover seemed to resonate with Christ's death: Jesus is the slaughtered lamb whose blood is shed to free his people from the bondage of sin.

The Holy Thursday service often includes another sacred rite instituted by Jesus on that eventful night. At the Last Supper, Jesus reminded his disciples that no one, no matter what their social status, was better than another. To demonstrate that, he—their master—knelt down before his disciples and performed the lowliest of tasks: He washed their feet.

These days, pastors might wash their parishioners' feet. Or the congregation may do it for each other. Even the pope is known to do this for homeless people on Holy Thursday, to demonstrate the equality and love that Christians profess. (In Britain, the monarch traditionally used to do this for the peasants. Nowadays the Queen does it symbolically, by giving ceremonial purses and coins to humble pensioners.)

The Holy Thursday service remembers another event from the Last Supper (John 13:31-34). This is when Jesus said: "A new commandment I give unto you." Because of this "commandment," Holy Thursday is known as "Maundy" Thursday—from the Latin *mandatum*, or "commandment." The new commandment was what some have called his greatest commandment, the one that sums up his entire message. On this night, he told his disciples: "Love one another as I have loved you."

Tintoretto, Christ Washing the Feet of the Disciples, c. 1575-80. On Maundy Thursday, Jesus gave his followers a new commandment: "Love one another as I have loved you." And then, washing the feet of his disciples, he walked the talk.

With the ritual of the Eucharist, or Holy Communion, Christians remember Jesus' Last Supper and the message of Easter.

The Maundy Thursday service concludes with the Eucharist or Holy Communion. As people take the bread and wine, they remember that first Passover meal. They remember the Last Supper meal. And they meditate on the ultimate sacrifice that Jesus was about to make on their behalf.

HOLY THURSDAY—PASSION ALL NIGHT LONG

The observance of Holy Thursday doesn't end at midnight. The most fervent continue on, following the events of the Passion after Jesus was arrested, when he faced a long night of arraignments, harsh interrogation, and abuse.

On Holy Thursday in Sevilla, the procession of floats and penitents peaks. The parade, featuring some of the most beloved and stirring floats, lasts from Thursday evening until Friday at dawn (giving the procession its Spanish name of *La Madrugá*, meaning "dawn").

The procession starts in silence and darkness with the brotherhood known as El Silencio. A small woodwind ensemble plays solemn music, announcing their arrival. Then the music stops, accentuating the utter silence. Penitents in all-black robes and pointed hats enter, accompanying a float with a statue of Jesus carrying his cross. The crowd stays silent as the float passes by, lit only by candles and the flickering of cell-phone cameras.

El Gran Poder—the statue whose hand was kissed by worshippers in the preceding days—also parades on this night. Bent over and lugging his long and heavy cross, Christ trudges in. Beneath him and hidden from view are the *costaleros* holding up the float—similarly bent over and trudging along.

In Andalucía, grand and emotional processions fill the streets as various floats illustrate scenes from the Passion.

La Macarena, the most beloved statue of Mary, enters. She's mourning her son, but her sorrow is a thing of beauty. She stands atop a golden float, under a canopy, dressed in white lace, with a golden halo behind her head. Before her are dozens of tall candles lighting her way. The candles flicker and the float sways, as La Macarena is carried along. Spectators lining the streets weep. From the crowd, a flamenco singer erupts in song—a mournful, trilling wail in the night that vocalizes the crowd's tortured emotions. The procession of La Macarena is the longest—from her home church to the cathedral and back—a total of 14 agonizing hours.

By the time dawn arrives, the penitents, worshippers, and float-bearing *costaleros* have undergone a major endurance test—experiencing just the tiniest slice of the agony their Lord had to suffer on this night so long ago.

GOOD FRIDAY

The Passion and Passion Plays

On Good Friday, the Passion is at its most passionate. The rituals of Easter intensify, with emotional church services. This was the day when Jesus was condemned, tortured, and crucified. Good Friday is not "Good" at all—the word comes from "God's" Friday.

A number of European communities remember the events of Jesus' final week by staging homegrown theatrical productions called Passion Plays. Ordinary folks pool their resources and prepare all year long for the chance to dress up in robes and sandals to play the roles.

The roots of Passion Plays date from earliest Christian times, when the faithful gathered to read the Bible story aloud. By medieval times, these liturgical readings had become rhymed and sung. They got a visual element, with people dressing in costume, posing in tableaus, and carrying symbolic objects. These are variously

Especially in Germany and Austria, Passion Plays vividly tell the story of Easter on stage.

known as mystery, miracle, or morality plays. As they became more dramatic, actors played a role, moved about on a specially-constructed stage, and exchanged dialogue. Passion Plays, focusing specifically on Christ's last days, grew out of this medieval tradition. In fact, Passion Plays (along with mystery/miracle/morality plays) were crucial in the development of modern theater. The cradle of most of these innovations was southern Germany and Austria.

Perhaps Europe's oldest and best-known Passion Play is performed in the small German town of Oberammergau. In 1633, the bubonic plague was sweeping across the land, killing as many as half the population of each town it hit. The people of Oberammergau promised God that if they were spared, they'd honor him with a grand Passion Play each decade in perpetuity. The town was seemingly miraculously spared, and for nearly 400 years, each decade, they honor their promise by putting on a Passion Play. The next performance is in 2020.

It's an epic undertaking. When you visit the town of Oberammergau in a year without the play, it's hard to understand how they pull it off. Oberammergau is a cutesy village of half-timbered homes, onion-domed churches, and woodworking shops. The town has only about 4,000 residents, but when the Play is approaching, everyone from the youngest to the oldest pitches in.

Oberammergau's Passion Play runs five hours long, and they perform it over a hundred times a season. It takes place in a huge hall (built in 1900) that seats 4,700 spectators and has a stage big enough to accommodate all the horses, oxen, props, and a cast of hundreds. Every 10 years, half a million people pour into tiny Oberammergau to catch a show. Despite the modern sound and lighting systems, the show keeps to the same text and same homespun fervor as was inaugurated four centuries ago in the face of the plague.

CANTIANO'S PASSION PLAY

While Oberammergau's is the most famous, there are similar (smaller-scale and less-touristed) productions throughout Europe—in Spain, the Netherlands, and the UK. Some theater companies have even recently revived long-lost mystery, miracle, morality, and Passion Plays.

One of my favorite places to see an authentic, homegrown Passion Play is in the tiny stone village of Cantiano in the mountains of Italy's remote Marche region. The village is picturesque without being cutesy, and the people are totally devoted.

As night falls, Cantiano's main square becomes a stage. Under a full moon in the crisp air, the entire village packs into the square to witness this timeless reenactment, just as they have for centuries. The town accountant dons a costume to become a centurion, the baker's wife becomes Pilate's wife, and the young IT whiz is this year's Jesus. Some people have played the same role for decades. Others play a succession of roles as they age—graduating from little-boy-in-the-crowd to Jesus to Jewish elder.

The townspeople consider it a great honor to play a part. It's an act of devotion.

In Italy's Marche region, the entire town of Cantiano becomes a stage set each Easter as it puts on its beloved Passion Play.

They personally go through the events of the Passion. At the end, they come out drained, like running an emotional marathon.

Cantiano uses the entire town as its stage. Jesus' trial takes place in the main square. But for the final climactic crucifixion scene, the entire cast trudges to the top of a nearby hill. Jesus is in the lead, carrying the cross. Meanwhile, the spectators remain below in the square, watching as the parade moves slowly up to the stark ridgeline above town, where three crosses stand silhouetted against the night sky. Witnessing the play—with its dramatic finale leaving the cross empty

but for a shroud blowing in the wind, floodlit on the summit of that hill—is an unforgettable and powerful experience.

SLOVENIAN PASSION PLAY

In Slovenia, the medieval town of Skofja Loka is famed for its Easter play. This version was written by a local monk in 1721 and has been performed ever since. There's a cast of literally a thousand locals along with 70 horses. The play unfolds in episodes, staged in various locations throughout the town, so the action comes from all sides, immersing the audience.

It's a departure from the standard version of the Passion. It's less a realistic narrative and more a medieval morality play—a mix that feels both primal and avant-garde. As well as Jesus and Pilate, the script includes symbolic and supernatural characters. The play is thought-provoking. When the mighty king and the humble cobbler appear, the audience has to ponder questions of equality. When a tormented soul is ravaged by devils, the whole audience also wonders—How will I choose to live my own life? But the most dramatic moments come when the play returns to the traditional narrative, and all eyes are on a suffering and dying Jesus.

Wherever they're staged, Passion Plays make the torturing of Jesus visceral. As told so vividly in the Bible, Jesus suffered greatly even before being nailed to the cross . . . stripped, humiliated, and whipped. At a Passion Play, you can see it right before your eyes—there he hangs, bloody and nearly naked in the bitter cold.

THE PASSION: JESUS' TRIAL

Passion Plays bring to life the events chronicled in the Bible. The account is found in the four books about the life of Jesus known as the Gospels. While the Gospels vary somewhat on specific details, the overall story is clear:

In the dark of night as Good Friday begins, Jesus is taken to the house of his main accuser, the high priest Caiaphas. Caiaphas, surrounded by other Jewish leaders, leads the interrogation.

They accuse Jesus of going around saying he's the long-prophesied leader anointed by God to restore the Jewish nation to greatness. They say he claimed to be the "Messiah" (a Hebrew word meaning the anointed one) or the "Christ" (the Greek translation), as well as the "Son of God" and "King of the Jews." Anyone making such wild claims would be guilty of the worst of crimes—of blasphemy and of recklessly inciting the people against the Jewish and Roman authorities.

The Bible makes it clear the whole proceeding is a kangaroo court. It's convened in secret, with sham witnesses, enhanced interrogation (Jesus is beaten), and not a hint of a Miranda warning. Through it all, Jesus remains silent. He's paraded before a series of Jewish authorities. They bring out witness after witness against Jesus. They urge him to answer and refute the charges (and unwittingly incriminate himself). Jesus says nothing.

Caiaphas keeps at it: "What do you say to all this? Have you no answer?" Jesus remains silent. Finally, Caiaphas is beside himself, and demands an answer: "Are you the Christ, the Son of God?!" he roars.

Jesus finally responds: "You have said so."

Caiaphas takes that as a confession. "He has blasphemed!" he yells to the court, tearing his clothes in outrage. "You've all heard it! What is your verdict?"

They all answer: "Guilty."

The Jewish leaders condemn Jesus to death. But the real power lies in the hands

of the Roman governor of Palestine, Pontius Pilate. So when morning arrives, they bring Jesus before Pilate. Pilate is skeptical of the Jewish leaders' accusations. "I find no evidence against him," he says. Even Pilate's wife urges him to let Jesus go, having had a disturbing dream about him.

Meanwhile, the Jewish leaders have drummed up a mob against Jesus, and Pilate fears a riot. So he addresses the rabble and allows them to choose one prisoner for release. "Who shall I release—Jesus or Barabbas?" The crowd, stirred up by the Jewish authorities, chooses the criminal Barabbas. "Then what shall I do with Jesus?" Pilate asks.

"Crucify him!"

As they lead Jesus away, Pilate takes a bowl of water, and washes his hands of the affair, telling everyone: "I am innocent of this man's blood. You take care of it yourselves!"

They take Jesus to be tortured, mocked, and humiliated. They strip him and put a purple robe around him. They braid a "crown" out of thorny vines and put it on his head. They put a "scepter" in his right hand. Kneeling before him, they mock him: "Hail, King of the Jews!" They spit on him and beat him on the head.

Then they lead him away to crucify him.

J. S. Bach's *Saint Matthew's Passion*—as the name implies—deals with Jesus' final days as described in the Bible's Book of Matthew (chapters 26 and 27). Bach specifically used Martin Luther's famous German translation of the Bible, the one that helped popularize what became the modern German language.

And the most famous oratorio of all—Handel's *Messiah*—was actually written for Eastertide, not Christmas. True, the first part is about Jesus' birth with tunes like "For unto us a child is born . . . and his name shall be called 'Wonderful, Counselor' . . . ." But the remainder of Handel's *Messiah* focuses on Easter themes—how Christ died for our sins ("Surely he hath borne our griefs . . .") and was resurrected ("I know that my Redeemer liveth . . .").

The *Messiah*'s earliest performances were during the Easter season. And its most famous tune reminded everyone of how Christ—having suffered abuse and

Music of the Passion

Some of history's great composers have been inspired to write music for Easter. Mozart wrote hymns for several old texts about Jesus' suffering on the cross *(Ave Verum Corpus and Davanti alla Croce)* that are still popular today, especially in Italy.

Two of classical music's most famous oratorios—J. S. Bach's *Saint Matthew's Passion* and Handel's *Messiah*—were written for the Easter season. (An oratorio is a series of songs around a single theme—a kind of "concept album"—written for choir, soloists, and orchestra.) Both oratorios debuted in the early 1700s and have been played regularly since.

death in the Passion—finally ascended triumphantly into heaven: "For the Lord God Omnipotent reigneth . . . And he shall reign forever and ever . . . King of Kings and Lord of Lords . . . Hallelujah!"

Europeans today still celebrate Easter with centuries-old compositions performed in churches by world-class choirs and orchestras. In America, we mark the season with the timeless 1950 classic—"Here Comes Peter Cottontail."

GOOD FRIDAY'S SACRED OBSERVANCES

Back in Cantiano, on Good Friday the predawn streets stir with young men. Their purpose: to awaken the town, telling everyone to gather at church. Why don't the church bells announce the morning, as they always do here? Because it's Good Friday, and on this day no bells ring.

Throughout Europe, churches are dressed in mourning. Church bells are cer-

Before dawn on Good Friday, Italian villagers in Cantiano wake their neighbors with the news of Jesus' Crucifixion, and then all gather in church.

emonially tied so they cannot ring. The bells will remain silent for the next two gloomy days. Inside churches, the crosses and religious art are draped in black or purple. For Good Friday, even the least-observant Catholics might avoid the forbidden meat of Lent, and have fish instead.

Church services are stark and somber, with little music or none at all. In monasteries (like Monte Oliveto Maggiore in Tuscany), monks chant to sanctify the day. Bible readings and sermons focus on the last utterances of Jesus as he hung dying on the cross. People pray silently. They leave in silence.

In many communities, they take their sadness to the streets. Good Friday is the day to follow a journey of devotion, one that mirrors Jesus' own troubled route. As they walk, they think of how Jesus trudged along with his cross to be crucified, punctuating the walk with prayers and remembrances of the Passion.

In Cantiano, this walk of devotion is the Procession of the Seven Churches, done in memory of the traditional seven places Jesus went from Thursday to Easter. The congregation gathers at their home church to pray. Then they head out,

Departed loved ones are not forgotten as the procession swings through the town cemetery, where each grave and burial niche has a flickering candle.

accompanied by a teenager carrying a cross draped in purple. As they walk, the priest prays and recites psalms. At the next church they pause for more prayers, before moving on again. The entire village converges on the town cemetery. Hundreds of candles illuminate both graves and burial niches. There, in this time of communal worship, the living remember their departed loved ones.

Nearby, in the medieval hill town of Gubbio, there's a procession of hooded penitents, similar to the ones in Sevilla. As they weave through the town's narrow, cobbled lanes, they carry crosses and candles. Each penitent's robe has a sewn-on cross, at chest height. They sing the *Miserere*, a musical setting of Psalm 51: "Have mercy on me, O God . . . ." The lament expresses the pain of the Crucifixion and the hope that it will "wash away all my iniquity and cleanse me from my sin." The men carry floats depicting Jesus bearing his cross and the Virgin Mary weeping. The holy statues rise high, as if floating above legions of mourners. Children carry

In the Italian town of Gubbio, hooded penitents parade, carrying symbols of Jesus' Crucifixion.

the tools of the Passion—hammers and nails. These are community heirlooms, a reminder that this ritual has been passed down—like the tools themselves—through many generations.

Elsewhere in Europe, the faithful follow a tradition called the Stations of the Cross (also called the Way of the Cross or the Via Crucis). These mark the 14 stops Jesus made on his way to his death—when he stumbles carrying his cross, meets his mother along the way, is comforted by a brave woman, is nailed to the cross, and so on. Many churches make it a simple indoor event, setting up paintings or crèche-like tableaus illustrating these events. People walk from stop to stop, contemplating each poignant event on that tragic day.

An epic-scale Stations of the Cross takes place at the Roman Colosseum. As night falls on Good Friday, thousands converge, pouring out of the Colosseo Metro stop. The pope himself presides, from a raised stage outside the Colosseum entrance. Floodlights illuminate the colossal structure, creating a dramatic backdrop. Choirs sing, altar boys parade with candles, and for each stop, a meditation is read. This custom has been held here since the 1700s, to honor the early Christian martyrs. Some scholars think that Christians were thrown to the lions in the Colosseum—dying bravely for their cause, just as their Lord had.

The Passion: Jesus' Crucifixion

According to the Gospels, Jesus was taken to a place called Golgotha—"The Place of the Skull." There, they crucified him. This barbaric execution technique—stripped naked, nailed to a cross, and left to die—was both excruciating and humiliating. Crucifixion was a Roman specialty, reserved only for the worst of the worst. When the rebel slave Spartacus dared to rise up against Roman rule (in 71 B.C.), the Romans crushed the revolt and lined the Appian Way with 6,000 crucified followers. Jesus posed a similar threat. As a pretender to the title of Messiah—the promised liberator of the Jewish nation—he needed to be made an example of.

The Bible doesn't flinch when it comes to the gruesome details: Jesus, having been beaten severely, is compelled to carry his own cross. It's an arduous journey, and Jesus is thankfully helped by good-hearted bystanders. When they reach Golgotha, the Roman soldiers strip him. They throw dice for possession of the soon-to-be-dead man's clothes. They nail him to the cross. He's crucified between two common criminals, with a mocking sign on his cross reading, "This is Jesus, the King of the Jews." (The sign is often abbreviated in artwork as I.N.R.I.: "Iesus of **N**azareth, **R**ex—king—of the **I**ews"; Latin uses "I" instead of "J.") As he hangs there, naked and slowly dying, Jesus is mocked mercilessly—by the soldiers, by passersby, even by one of the criminals. When he cries out in thirst, they give him sour wine.

Through it all, Jesus is stoic and loving. He assures the criminal next to him he'll soon be in paradise. He assures his mother she'll be cared for. Of the people who have abused him so badly, he prays, "Father, forgive them, for they know not what they do." Then he cries out with a loud voice: "Father, into your hands I commend my spirit." And finally—"It is finished."

Sandro Botticelli,
Lamentation over the
Dead Christ, *1490-92*

SATURDAY

THE WORLD WAITS

THIS IS THE DAY Christ lay in the tomb, while his disciples mourned, lost without their leader. Even though Jesus had told them that he would be "killed, and on the third day be raised," the disciples hadn't fully grasped what he meant. Like the disciples, devout Christians today spend Holy Saturday in mournful limbo. It's an intentionally calm day, with no major events or church services planned. They spend the time mourning . . . and waiting.

As evening falls, they may attend an informal service called the Easter Vigil. It lasts from dusk until midnight or later—for the hardcores it can last all through the night until dawn. Very little happens. The church is often dark, lit only by candles. There's little or no hymn-singing. Worshippers pray and meditate to themselves, or might occasionally chant together: "We wait on the Lord. He is our light

In Germanic countries, Easter Saturday is the day of the "Easter Fire," a tradition that goes back to pagan times. Winter is metaphorically tossed onto the flames as people await the return of spring.

in darkness." Mostly, they sit. They wait patiently for the coming of the next day, when—hopefully—Jesus will be resurrected, as he promised.

In Germanic countries, there's a completely different way to mark Saturday night, with a ritual rooted in timeless pagan traditions. As darkness falls, people gather on hillsides—neo-pagans, Christians, and anyone who loves beer—to build an "Easter Fire." To light the fire, they may even use their old dry Christmas tree. Throughout the night, they stoke the fire, drink, sing, and make a lot of rowdy noise. Like the Druids of old, they metaphorically toss winter into the flames, and await the coming of spring.

GREECE—THE EASTERN ORTHODOX EASTER

Eastern Orthodox Christians celebrate Easter exactly like Catholics and Protestants in the West . . . except that they do it on a completely different Sunday . . . and they have totally different rituals . . . and they also make Saturday into a huge deal . . . and they eat lamb-intestine stew.

The differences between the Eastern and Western branches of Christianity are a result of 2,000 years of geopolitical separation. In the fourth century, the ancient Roman Empire split in two, with two political rulers (in Rome and Constantinople/Istanbul) and two religious leaders (the pope and the patriarch). The divide hardened in the Great Schism of 1054, when the pope and patriarch excommunicated each other.

As the two cultures continued on their separate trajectories, their Easter celebrations developed different rituals. The Eastern world stuck with the old Julian calendar (see page 33), so they now celebrate Easter on a different Sunday—usually a week or two after the West. Greeks call the holiday *Pascha* (from the Greek word for Passover). And for them, Easter—not Christmas—is far and away the most important holy day of the year, the "Feast of Feasts."

Holy Saturday is just as big as Sunday. In the Orthodox tradition, Saturday

was the day when Jesus—having died—journeyed to hell to minister to those souls waiting there. The Saturday church services are part of a multiday celebration that spans the three days leading up to Easter Sunday.

The Ritual Begins

The Orthodox Easter service is a symbolic funeral, burial, and resurrection of Christ. The events transpire over several days, from Thursday to Sunday, with one service seeming to blend into the other. Churches remain open pretty much 24/7, and worshippers stream in and out as they can.

As worshippers enter their church (whether for Easter or any time of year), they follow a certain routine:

They drop a coin into a wooden donation box by the door and pick up a candle. They light the candle, place it on a rack of candles, say a prayer, make the sign of the cross, and kiss the nearby icon. They enter the nave, whose walls are decorated with icons—pictures of saints on golden backgrounds. The main icon shows Christ triumphant—seated on a throne and giving a blessing, in his role as the Pantocrator, or "Ruler of All." But during Holy Week, icons are added to the center of the church, depicting Christ being crucified on the cross, then after the Crucifixion, showing the cross alone.

The worshippers find a place to stand, not sit, as Eastern Orthodox churches generally have no pews (except for the infirm). They believe standing empowers prayers. Men stand on one side and women on the other.

As the service unfolds, there's always lots of spectacle, to enhance the religious experience. The priest wears a long black robe and a tall hat. He typically has a long beard—a sign of wisdom, experience, and respect. He periodically retreats

In Greek Orthodox tradition, Good Friday and Easter Saturday are busy with long and emotional services. It's as if the entire community is attending the funeral of a lost loved one. Jesus—on the cross and then off— is bedecked with flowers.

behind an icon-covered wall called an iconostasis, which marks off an especially holy space. Then, after blessing the Communion wafers or doing other spiritual heavy-lifting, he emerges again to circulate among the congregation.

For Easter services, the church is specially decorated. Beautifully-decorated ostrich eggs dangle from the chandeliers. The church is draped in lots of mourning purple.

The service is not complete without lots and lots of incense. This helps involve all the senses. There are different scents for different occasions, each one conveying a different emotional message—the agony of the Passion or the ecstasy of Resurrection. The Orthodox service is less about long sermons and intellectual ideology. It's about experiencing God's mysteries. The incense is crucial in this. It's said of non-believers and skeptics that their problem is only that they have "not yet experienced the incense."

Requiem for a Deity

The marathon Orthodox Easter service is basically a symbolic funeral for Jesus. Just as the disciples readied Jesus for burial, the faithful prepare his tomb. It begins on the morning of Good Friday, when women flock to their parish church to decorate the symbolic tomb, or coffin. It can be as simple as a plywood box or an elaborate canopy. They decorate the exterior with flowers, and also sprinkle flower petals inside as a resting place.

Then comes the burial. An image of Christ—usually a flat wooden icon affixed to the wall—is removed from the cross. His "body" is then carried behind the iconostasis. As candles flicker, worshippers chant and pray together, awaiting the next step as the story unfolds. A cantor sings and leads the congregation and choir, to add another element to the atmosphere of reverence.

Eventually the priest re-emerges carrying the image of Jesus wrapped in a shroud. This cloth represents how the crucified Christ was wrapped for burial. He reverently leads it through the congregation of mourners. The precious and

The symbolic casket holding Jesus is draped with flowers and carried from the church in a funeral procession that winds slowly through town.

now carefully folded shroud is laid in the coffin—the ceremonial coffin. Other symbolic objects are placed in the coffin. The image of Jesus on the shroud is lovingly decked in flowers. As in any funeral, loved ones file by to pay their last respects with a kiss. The Orthodox mysticism—enhanced by music, incense, and tears—heightens the emotional impact.

The ritual of mourning continues throughout the day. As dusk arrives, the funeral procession starts. The coffin is lifted onto broad shoulders and carried out of the church. All over town, other churches are simultaneously performing the same funeral rituals—carrying their individual coffins through town. The parades converge on the main square, where it seems the entire population awaits. The bishop, flanked by the town's priests, gives an Easter message—reminding his flock why Jesus died and why there's reason for hope. For the most fervent faithful, the service continues all night long.

On Saturday, worshippers pack their church yet again. Saturday is the longest Orthodox service of the entire year. This is to remember how, while his disciples were mourning on earth, convinced that Jesus was gone for good, Jesus was continuing his mission. On this day he descended into hell, bringing salvation to the souls of the righteous dead (like Adam and Eve) who were awaiting resurrection. This event is not in the Bible, though it's alluded to in Matthew 27:52-53. It's been immortalized in the Apostles' Creed that is recited regularly by Catholics and Protestants alike, who profess their belief that, "He descended into hell . . . ."

Symbolically, this is the pivotal moment when Christ defeated the devil and death. Greeks call Saturday "The First Resurrection." But even though Christ has conquered death, he himself is still dead, so there is no mention yet that Christ is "risen."

Greek Orthodox priests often sport a long beard, a symbol of wisdom.

The priest changes out of his mournful black vestments and into hopeful white ones. Much happier and more animated, he tosses dried flower petals over his parishioners. This lets them know that Christ has accomplished his task—the chains of hell and death have been broken, and new life is on the way.

The people spill from their churches and once again fill the main square in town. This time, the mood is lighter—there's a palpable sense of expectation. Easter Sunday is on its way.

SATURDAY NIGHT VIGIL

It's been weeks and weeks of buildup: from the planning of Carnival in November (*"am elften Elften um elf Uhr elf"*) to the wanton partying of Fat Tuesday (Mardi

In the Greek town of Nafplio, everyone gathers on the main square on Saturday night. At the stroke of midnight, fireworks fill the sky and Easter Sunday arrives. People share the kiss of love, light candles, and declare "He is risen!"—and then head home for a midnight feast.

Gras). Ash Wednesday ushered in the 40 days of fasting, prayer, and reflection of Lent. During Holy Week, worshippers waved palms, kissed holy statue toes, hefted floats, chanted in churches, and donned robes and sandals for local Passion Plays.

Meanwhile, the kids have dyed and painted Easter eggs. Parents have decorated their homes with lilies, daffodils, pussy willows, and fake grass. Grandma and grandpa have been invited to stay the night (so dad is sleeping on the couch). Moms have spent the week browsing the open-air markets for hams, lambs, and all kinds of candy and chocolates. They've baked their *semlas*, fried their *torrijas*, and crossed their buns with hot frosting. The Easter dress is ironed, the kids bathed, and the eggs blessed.

Now, it's Saturday night. In Germany, little kids are setting out their Easter nests hoping that the Easter Hare will come during the night and fill it with goodies. French children do the same, in the hopes that flying Easter Bells will bring them chocolate Easter fish. In Holland, young revelers are welcoming in spring with bonfires and Heinekens. In Spain, a float depicting Mary mourning her dead son is carried slowly through the streets. In Greece, villagers gather in the main square to light candles from a holy flame. In Italy, playful family members prepare to surprise loved ones with a special gift inside a chocolate egg. And in churches across Europe, the faithful gather for meditative vigils to await what comes next.

Meanwhile, in that timeless realm of the spiritual world, Jesus lies dead and buried in his tomb, with a big and ominous stone rolled across the entrance.

EASTER SUNDAY

BANG! IT'S EASTER!

As a new day dawns on Easter Sunday, the mood changes instantly.

Easter starts with a bang in Greece, as soon as the clock strikes midnight. Bang! Pow! Whoosh! Fireworks light up the sky. The crowd that has gathered on the town square joyously lights candles. They get their light from their neighbor, then pass it along. The flame originated in Jerusalem's Church of the Holy Sepulchre (which traditionally marks the site of Jesus' Crucifixion), was flown on a jet to Athens, then distributed throughout Greece. As ordinary Greeks receive the flame and light each other's fire, they happily exchange the ritual Easter "kiss of love." The whole scene feels more like a happy New Year's Eve than pious Easter.

In Italy, the city of Florence also starts off Easter Sunday with fireworks. The tradition, dating from medieval times, is known as the Scoppio del Carro—the

For centuries in Florence, Easter Sunday morning has been celebrated with special medieval pageantry.

"Explosion of the Cart." The parade starts just after sunrise with the sound of a stately drum beat echoing through the narrow streets. Men march dressed in colorful tights and medieval doublets. With much pomp and pageantry, they wave flags, twirl them, and toss them in the air. A team of white oxen lumbers along, pulling an unusual wooden wagon—a tall, pagoda-like thing. It's colorfully painted red, blue, and gold, and covered with mysterious symbols—dolphins, castles, garlands, coats-of-arms, and a big sun. The parade comes to a halt at the religious center of Florence, midway between the historic Duomo (cathedral) and the equally historic Baptistery. A crowd has gathered, filled with anticipation. Dads perch daughters on their shoulders for a better look. Nearby balconies are filled with lucky residents and their invited friends. TV cameras on cranes and booms pivot overhead, angling for the best shot for the live broadcast.

Medieval pageantry culminates with a literal bang as people gather on the doorstep of the cathedral for the annual "Explosion of the Cart."

Inside the church, they've been saying a Mass. When Mass ends, the celebration begins. Church bells start ringing. Then a mechanical dove representing the Holy Spirit rockets from the high altar. It zips along a wire, directly out the door, and crashes into the cart.

Bang! Fireworks erupt. Suddenly the cart is a pyrotechnic launch pad, emitting showers of sparks, crackling firecrackers, whooshing bottle rockets, spinning pinwheels, whistling noisemakers, and lots and lots and lots of blue smoke. It's a spectacular way to announce the Resurrection and a joyous start to Easter Sunday. And after the last fireworks explode, the fire marshal checks the cart to make sure this year's Scoppio really *is* over.

In Rome, Easter Sunday worshippers pack into St. Peter's Square at the Vatican for a Mass with the pope.

CHRIST IS RISEN

On this morning the faithful everywhere fill churches, declaring with great joy: "Christ is risen . . . He is risen indeed—Alleluia!" They celebrate the Resurrection and the promise of salvation.

At the Vatican, St. Peter's Square is filled with more than 100,000 people from around the world, plus a global audience watching on TV. They've gathered at the spot where an Easter Sunday Mass has been said for 1,700 years. As the Mass begins, the pope ceremonially greets the Risen Christ by kissing a much-venerated icon of Christ as Pantocrator. (This ancient rite fell into disuse in the 14th century, but has been revived in the 21st century.) After the Mass, the pope steps out onto the grand balcony of St. Peter's Basilica. With the wide-angle expanse of St. Peter's facade as his backdrop, he delivers his famous blessing to "the City and the World"—*"Urbi et Orbi."*

Raphael,
The Transfiguration,
1516-20

All over Europe, in churches grand and small, Easter is a time to make an appearance at church. For some people, it may be their only church visit all year.

The Easter Sunday service focuses on the wonder of the Resurrection, as related in the Bible:

After Jesus was crucified, his body was taken down from the cross, and lovingly wrapped by his followers in linen and anointed with spices. They laid the body in a new tomb cut out of rock, and a large stone was rolled in front of the entrance. The Jewish leaders—remembering Jesus' prophecies that he would rise again after three days—demanded that soldiers be sent to guard the tomb.

At dawn on Easter Sunday, the women who followed Jesus (including Mary Magdalene) arrived at the tomb to anoint the body. They found the rock rolled away and a young man (an angel) sitting there, whose clothes were as white as

LEFT *Matthias Grünewald, Resurrection, c. 1515*

RIGHT *Titian, Noli me Tangere, c. 1514. Jesus rockets from the tomb in a cosmic explosion of Resurrection joy, knocking the Roman guards silly. Later, when Jesus' followers find him alive, they have a hard time believing their eyes.*

snow. "Don't be afraid," the angel said, "He has been raised. Go tell his disciples." The women were—to quote the various Bible accounts—"terribly frightened," "perplexed," and full of "bewilderment," "fear," and "great joy."

As they ran to tell the disciples, Jesus met them. "Greetings!" he said. "Do not be afraid. Go and tell my brothers they will see me."

The women continued on and told the disciples they'd seen Jesus. The disciples did not believe them, as it "seemed to be nonsense." Only Peter got up and ran to the tomb, and found it empty.

Over the course of the next weeks, Jesus appeared to many more people: to Peter, to followers near Emmaus (where he ate a meal with them), to his 11 disciples, and even to a crowd of more than 500. He told them, "Don't be afraid," and assured them he wasn't a ghost but a real person. "Touch me and see," he said. Even the disciple who came to be nicknamed Doubting Thomas was convinced once he put his finger in Jesus' wounds.

After 40 days, Jesus gathered his disciples on a mountaintop. He told them to go and preach the good news to the whole world. He assured them: "I am with you always." Then he blessed them and was taken up into heaven.

HALLELUJAH, CHURCH IS OVER!

After church, everyone heads home—for family, friends, food, and fun. Now Easter belongs to the kids. Even if they're too young to understand how the egg symbolizes resurrection and rebirth, they certainly know the excitement of an Easter egg hunt.

In Europe (just as in America) kids scramble to find hidden Easter eggs and candy. They grab their wicker Easter basket or pail or bag and have at it. They search the backyard (if they have one), in the house, or at a community gathering in the town park. The eggs may be hidden by the Easter Hare (Germany), the Easter Bunny (Britain), the Easter Bells (France), or by the Easter Mom and Dad.

Christ the Lord is Risen Today

Music is a big part of the Easter church service, a joyful way to celebrate the Resurrection. One of the most popular Easter hymns in Britain (and America) is the rousing "Christ the Lord Is Risen Today."

The lyrics were written by Charles Wesley (1708-1788) who, along with his brother John, was one of the founders of Methodism. Charles wrote more than 6,000 hymns, convinced that singing was a form of worship. He wrote this hymn as a young man (in 1739), but it

wasn't until a century later that the hymn really took off. Now it's a staple for choirs and congregations to sing as the Easter Sunday service begins.

The buoyant music for Charles' words comes from an earlier hymn (by an unknown composer). And the song's most distinctive element—the word "Alleluia"—was not in Charles' original. Someone added it later (praise God!), giving us the stirring refrain that gets everyone singing: "Ah-ah-ah-ah-aah-lay-loo-oo-yah!"

Christ, the Lord, is risen today, Alleluia!
Sons of men and angels say, Alleluia!
Raise your joys and triumphs high, Alleluia!
Sing, ye heavens, and earth, reply, Alleluia!

Lives again our glorious King, Alleluia!
Where, O death, is now thy sting? Alleluia!
Once He died our souls to save, Alleluia!
Where thy victory, O grave? Alleluia!

Hail, the Lord of earth and heaven, Alleluia!
Praise to Thee by both be given, Alleluia!
Thee we greet triumphant now, Alleluia!
Hail, the Resurrection, thou, Alleluia!

King of glory, Soul of bliss, Alleluia!
Everlasting life is this, Alleluia!
Thee to know, Thy power to prove, Alleluia!
Thus to sing and thus to love, Alleluia!

It's a mad scramble to find as many eggs as possible as quickly as possible. And, as is so often the case, the tearful little ones who miss out get a little extra love.

Some cultures (and families) have their own quirky kinds of fun. There might be egg-rolling contests, to see whose rolls farthest. Or egg-tossing contests, to see whose egg cracks first and whose survives. Or brother and sister tap eggs together, trying to crack each other's egg.

Besides eggs, the kids find other goodies left overnight by their particular gift-giving creature. In Germany, kids might find that their nest is now full of candies or pastries shaped like the *Osterhase* (Easter Hare) or the *Osterlämmchen* (Easter Lambkin). In Denmark, children find a bare branch that's now filled with candy leaves; they wake up their sleepy parents by whacking them with it. (Czech kids have a similar branch-whipping custom.) In Italy, kids and adults alike find a big, hollow chocolate egg with a special gift inside.

As the kids squeal with excitement, parents and grandparents look on, recalling Easter celebrations from their own childhoods.

Through the lands, hunting for candy eggs is the first Easter memory for many tiny ones.

Let the Feast Begin

While every culture and every family has their own unique Easter traditions, there's one common denominator—food.

Friends and family gather together for a big meal and lots of convivial socializing. This is when extended families—three or four generations, cousins, and in-laws—might make their annual or semi-annual contact. In most of Europe, Easter Sunday spills into Easter Monday—both are public holidays. So there may be two big meals—Sunday at mom's parents' and Monday at dad's. It's a time for eating, catching up, and taking walks together. After the fasting of Lent, the solemn church services, intense Passion rituals, and all the prep work, now is the time to simply kick back and enjoy. It seems the gift of Easter and the promise of spring brings out a deep-seated urge to gather loved ones together and embrace life to its fullest.

For the main meal, it seems that every culture (and family) has its signature

dishes. The French love leg of lamb. Brits have an affinity for ham, and it's herring in Scandinavia. Almost everywhere, eggs grace the table in some form—hard-boiled, in a soup as a starter course, or as painted eggs to be used in colorful centerpieces. Some families make sure the Easter menu has been thoroughly blessed by the priest the day before. Every culture makes a big deal of dessert—there's no end of special cakes and pastries, and lots of chocolate eggs and candy.

In Greece, the feasting starts just after midnight. After the Saturday night fireworks and candle-sharing, everyone hurries home for a meal. As they enter they raise their candle up, making a cross above their doorway to bless their home for the coming year.

Then they sit down for their Easter meal—their *first* one. It's a festive family gathering. The star attraction is a traditional thick soup made of lamb entrails called *magiritsa*. They also devour lots of hard-boiled eggs (dyed red to symbolize

Christ's blood) and meat and Easter breads, as the feast continues into the wee hours of Easter Sunday. A much-loved contest is to crack eggs with others; the lucky one whose egg stays intact will have an especially blessed year.

As the sun rises, the feasting doesn't stop—it's an all-day affair. The men start stoking the coals, preparing a barbecue. They grill a spring lamb on a spit for the afternoon meal. This goes on in backyards and town squares all over Greece. To round out the menu, *kokoretsi* is also on the spit. This beloved specialty—lamb organ meat wrapped carefully in intestines and roasted to moist perfection—assures that nothing is wasted. It takes hours to get the roasting done just right—but no one's in a hurry.

The barbecue is an excuse for a party. There's lots of drinking, singing, and dancing. There's the traditional "burning of Judas"—when an effigy of the disgraced betrayer is set in flames with much rejoicing. In villages all across Greece, families are grilling lamb, going from house to house through the neighborhood to check on other people's lambs, sharing drinks, and socializing. When the spit finally stops turning, the next meal begins: lamb off the bone, lamb off the knife, lamb off the fingers, beer, Easter bread, wine, music, more food, more fun, more lamb. People party into the night.

Eventually the whole village ends up back at the church, dancing and singing. Together they celebrate Easter and the hope of renewal—as they have every year all their lives.

THREE GENERATIONS AND A STRANGER

I had the great privilege of sharing an Easter meal with a family in rural Tuscany. It's in remote villages that sacred traditions—rich with symbolism—survive most vividly. *Nonna* (grandma) runs the kitchen as the meal is prepared. She

Coming home with their Easter candle after midnight—as Easter Sunday arrives—this Greek family scorches a cross above their door to bless their home for the coming year.

makes the special holiday rolls, called *ciambelle*. With a gentle touch, she kneads the dough, then shapes it into rings, representing the crown of thorns.

The eight-year-old takes them out to grandfather, who's busy stoking the oven with wood from his olive trees. When the coals are just right he spreads them carefully. Drawing from the practice of a lifetime of Easters, he cooks the *ciambelle* to perfection. In his cellar, he cuts a cured pork salami, hung from the rafters there to dry specially for this Easter meal.

As all generations gather, the feast begins. Grandfather blesses the occasion with a toast. He slices his prized salami ceremonially like a Thanksgiving turkey. Eggs that have been blessed by the village priest are now passed around to be eaten, along with a wide variety of homemade breads. The main course is roast baby lamb served with a special, egg-based Easter soup (*Brodetto Pasquale*). The tagliatelle pasta has been made from scratch by grandma, mom, and the girls. For dessert, the *ciambelle* are served along with a small glass of a special dessert wine

Throughout the lands and across the centuries, people lovingly pass traditions—what they eat, how they party, and how they pray—from one generation to the next.

called vin santo—"Holy Wine"—recalling the body and blood of Jesus. Our bellies stuffed, we take a late-afternoon walk through the village.

I know that my experience in Tuscany is one that is shared by people all across Europe. Everywhere, extended—yet close-knit—families are pulling out all the holiday stops. The table is set with their precious family heirlooms. The dishes are lovingly prepared and familiar to all.

On Easter Sunday, it seems that everyone has a place to be. And on this particular Easter, I'm fortunate to be with friends in this Tuscan farmhouse. To be

With each spring, the promise of life renewed is affirmed.

so far from my own home and loved ones yet feel so welcome with this family is a memory I'll treasure for the rest of my Easters.

The Timeless Cycle of Birth and Rebirth

Let the bells ring—Easter is the joyous day of Resurrection, when Jesus rose from the dead. And more, it's the season of rebirth. Flowers trumpet the bloom of spring, and the earth reawakens from its winter slumber. The daffodils and pussy willows appear in the northern countries, the jacarandas in Spain, and the lilacs and bougainvillea in Greece. Locals say nature is racing hard to try to celebrate the Resurrection before the people do. It's a new day, filled with promise, both spiritually and metaphorically.

The Easter season is also a time to reflect on the seasons of life, as parents, grandparents, and children celebrate. It's a chance to bask in the timeless glow of families and communities coming together, to remember the importance of loved ones in our lives, and to pass traditions on to the next generation.

By highlighting Europe's vivid holiday traditions—from crazy Carnival to penitential Lent, from the sadness of Holy Week to the joy of Easter morning—we've seen the richness of the human experience exemplified within the season. Easter is complex yet simple, tied to a time yet timeless. Birth and rebirth—the cycle continues.

With two crews filming Easter in five countries, we got up close and intimate with family traditions—as in Greece, where godchildren visit their godparents to enjoy quality time dyeing eggs.

THE MAKING OF THE *RICK STEVES'* *EUROPEAN EASTER* SPECIAL

BACK IN 2014, we set our sights on capturing Europe's unique Easter traditions in a one-hour public television special and this companion book. Our mission: to give viewers a seat at the family feast, a pew right up front, and a look at the joy of the season through the eyes of everyday kids, parents, and pilgrims.

It was a bit daunting. How could we possibly cover such a diverse variety of customs—Christian, pagan, secular, and edible—in so many different countries?

I turned to my eyes-and-ears in Europe: the tour guides I work with. I challenged them to make a case for why their country should be featured. The range of customs I got in response astounded me, shattering my preconceived notions of what "Easter" was all about.

I wanted to show European traditions that would appeal equally to Christians, non-Christians, and to anyone with a thirst for culture, history, and the variety of the human experience. I looked for rituals that would resonate with American families whose ancestors had emigrated from Europe. And, as commercialization has driven out much of the wonder of our sacred holidays, I was eager to seek out remote communities where old traditions remain strong.

Sorting through the many possibilities, I zeroed in on the places I thought would make the most compelling television. In spite of my Protestant Scandinavian heritage, I found myself drawn to southern Catholic and Orthodox cultures, where people seemed to celebrate with

special fervor. Their customs seemed the most pure (unchanged through time), and many of their traditions dated back to medieval, ancient, and even prehistoric times.

For the next year, we made our plans, and eventually came up with a working script. Rather than try to cover the European Easter geographically, we decided to tell the story chronologically. We'd follow the entire Easter season, from raucous Carnival to somber Lent to the Passion Story of Holy Week to the joy of Easter Sunday. In a more general sense, Easter is also the story of how winter turns to spring and sorrow is transformed into rebirth.

My tour-guide colleagues laid out the dates and times when their culture celebrated the season most colorfully. Then I sat down to design an itinerary that would result in a maximum dose of Easter. At first it seemed like a logistical nightmare. Fortunately, itinerary planning is a Rubik's Cube I actually enjoy solving.

For example, how could we be four places at once, trying to film Easter Sunday in four different countries? Fortunately for us, Greeks observe Easter Sunday a week later, so with a little planning, we could film one Easter Sunday in Italy, then fly to Greece for the next. And in Spain, we'd skip Easter Sunday and film Palm Sunday instead (which is a bigger deal), and still have time to get to Slovenia for their Easter Sunday. And so on. With two film crews and a good itinerary, we hoped to shoot four Easters, three Carnivals in three different countries, and several different families as they marked traditions through the Easter season.

We booked our flights, checked train connections, and reserved a rental van.

During our shoot, we worked in Spain, Switzerland, Slovenia, Italy, and Greece.

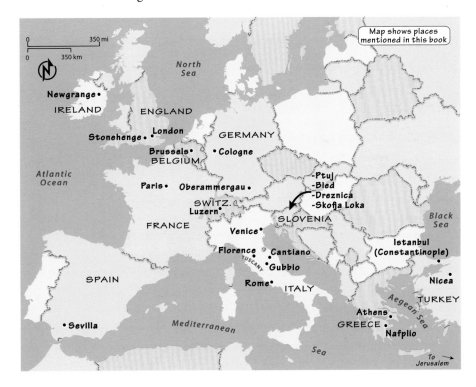

We received filming permission from various museums, choirs, and churches. I hired a guide from each of the chosen countries to be our local expert and "fixer." The guides got busy making arrangements with families who'd be willing to let us crash their celebrations with cameras in tow.

THE FILM CREW— "GETTING THE BAND BACK TOGETHER"

For the film crew, I'm fortunate to have some of the best in the business. I like working with a small, mobile, guerrilla-style crew. We set up fast, film whatever's

On Palm Sunday, producer Simon Griffith and cameraman Karel Bauer (shown here perched high above St. Peter's Square) got dressed up to see the pope.

happening now, and move on. We schlep all our own gear. It takes a special talent to do this kind of work. You have to be both an artist as well as a hardy, roll-with-it traveler.

The crew consisted of me, producer/director Simon Griffith, and cameraman Karel Bauer. The three of us have traveled together as a team for many years, through many different countries, and filmed dozens of shows.

We could never have pulled off this Easter special without Simon Griffith. Simon has overseen both the production in the field and the editing back home of every show I've hosted for nearly 20 years. He and I have forged a close working relationship, having spent over 600 days together on the European road. Simon makes all the necessary arrangements beforehand, helps shape the focus of the shows, and works with me doing last-minute on-the-spot rewrites. Our videographer Karel Bauer has shot more than half of my shows, and must be one of the country's most well-traveled photographers.

The three of us work together on every aspect of the shoot: Over dinner we're planning the next day's schedule; at breakfast, we're talking about how to shoot a particular scene; on the road, we're debating what I'm going to say when the cameras roll, and how the shot will look. Our years of experience of working and traveling together have made us (if I may modestly say) one of the most efficient television crews anywhere.

For this particular project, we knew we'd need a second crew. Valerie Griffith, the second crew field producer, had also worked on our earlier Christmas special. For the Easter production, Valerie helped shape the script, and worked closely with our European guides to set up locations and schedules ahead of time. Conveniently, Valerie is also the spouse of Simon Griffith, and the two producers were constantly in touch throughout the shoot. They could monitor which elements were turning out strong and which were weak, so the next crew could fill the gaps. (For more on Val and her crew, see page 190.)

THE SHOOT

As 2015 dawned, we were ready to film. We started in the depths of winter with Carnival. The scheduling was in our favor. We hit Venice first, because they start partying early. Then we moved on to Slovenia, whose most-colorful rituals are a couple of days later. This gave the crew just enough time to get to Switzerland to film the finale of Carnival on Fat Tuesday. On their flight home, the crew fit in a quick stop in London. At the National Gallery they filmed paintings by many great masters—from Duccio to Titian to Rubens—which we could use to tell the Bible story of Christ through beautiful art.

So far, so good.

We spent the 40 days and 40 nights of Lent back in the States planning the next, more-complicated phase of shooting. In April, our two crews headed to Europe again for Palm Sunday.

The filming intensity really ratcheted up during Holy Week. There was something happening every single day all over Europe. We were determined to follow the week day by day, to show how Europeans mark the season as it builds in anticipation of Easter Sunday. This meant a lot of tight schedules, and lots of frequent-flyer hopping from country to country, to capture each culture at its most vivid celebration.

We had to divide and conquer, sending Val's crew to Spain and Slovenia, while Simon, Karel, and I did Italy and Greece.

We were in Rome for Palm Sunday—just us, the pope, and 120,000 others. Having the gravitas of the Vatican and the stately High Church ritual on St. Peter's Square was an important element of the show. Simon and Karel negotiated the crowds to get great shots of the waving sea of palm branches and red-robed dignitaries.

We wanted to complement that grand-scale High Church ceremony with a rustic small-town Italian Easter. Monday, Tuesday, and Wednesday were perfect for that, as there was less church activity. So we focused on families preparing for the upcoming festivities.

Roberto Bechi, our Sienese guide, was brilliant at lining up both secular and religious traditions for us to film. (All of the guides I mention are excellent, and are recommended in my guidebooks. They're longtime collaborators, helping with our bus tours and my research.) Roberto has a special passion for local cuisine, which gave us great insight into holiday feasting. We had fun experiences watching Italian mamas make pasta by hand and special Easter treats being passed down through the generations. We saw the shine in kids' eyes as they looked forward to Easter egg hunts and chocolate eggs on Easter Sunday.

We explored more of Italy's hill towns. While I know Rome and Tuscany well,

Our Easter show would not have been possible without the expert support of our wonderful local guides: Concepción Delgado (in Sevilla, Spain), Marijan Krišković (in Slovenia), Patti Staikou (in Nafplio, Greece), and Roberto Bechi (shown here with our crew—me, Simon, and Karel on Herod's throne).

venturing into Italy's Marche region was a first for me. I particularly enjoyed the town of Cantiano with its Passion Play. I'm glad to be able to give these warm and wonderful people a wider audience. Throughout the Italian countryside, we visited small churches and got to see humble services and devoted choirs. It was especially moving to see the straightforward way they celebrated Holy Thursday (The Last Supper and Jesus washing his disciples' feet) and Good Friday (Jesus' betrayal and Crucifixion).

SPECIAL CHALLENGES

Filming church services in action needs to be done sensitively. We met with the pastors and priests beforehand to explain our work and how we hoped to share the worshipping with our public television viewers in a thoughtful and respectful way. Generally they welcomed us and our camera to capture the action they were so passionate about.

Filming Easter required lots of shooting in the dark—dim churches, bonfires at night, and mysterious candlelit ceremonies. Thankfully, on the eve of the shoot we purchased a new, amazingly light-sensitive camera. We were able to capture scenes that would have been un-shootable with the existing technology just a year prior. Many times during the shoot, producer Simon marveled to me that without our new camera, certain scenes would have simply been impossible.

Because of our jam-packed schedule of celebrations, we had to do lots of improvising. Early on, I'd drafted a working script and built our schedule around programs suggested by each of our guides. But as we went, we were constantly balancing things, rewriting, rescheduling, and then finessing it all into a workable plan.

Lots of things didn't pan out. We'd hoped to find more secular traditions— Easter Bunnies and such—but because we were focusing on the more devout corners of Europe, we found plenty of sacred and not much secular.

Filming families during intimate celebrations was another balancing act. We didn't want to intrude on their family time, or change the dynamic by our presence, or turn it into some stagey collection of folk clichés. Fortunately, our guides always made us feel welcome and our friendly crews have lots of experience at blending in. I've found that most Europeans—even grandmas and grandpas—are quick to get over the glare of the camera and focus on their families.

With the latest technology, our video cameras could shoot by candlelight. And for many of the rituals we saw, that's all the light there was.

Filming in Sevilla and Slovenia
by Valerie Griffith

Stark contrast defined my crew's two experiences: Our Easter shoot in Sevilla was an intense, euphoric, crowded assault on the senses. Slovenia was a quiet journey to an unspoiled land.

No amount of research or Googling could prepare me for Holy Week in Sevilla. It is, in a word, sensuous. The spring air, perfumed with orange blossoms and sandalwood incense, is intoxicating. Our nights were lit by thousands of candles as dreamy statues of Mary floated by, rose petals rained down, and a steady heartbeat of drums and wail of trumpets drifted above the city. We definitely weren't in Kansas anymore.

On the other hand, trying to film it all was a nightmare. We had to negotiate overwhelming crowds to capture an impossibly varied array of events.

Fortunately, we had an experienced crew. Our local guide, the superb Concepción Delgado, brilliantly used her know-how to move us quickly through streets jammed with surging crowds. Our cameraman, Peter Rummel, is a seasoned hand, having shot almost all of Rick's shows that Karel Bauer didn't. (Each man's videographic style is unique—it's fun to watch Rick's shows and play "Spot the Difference.") Peter had to thread through the crowds, carrying his camera and tripod, all while planning

Producer Val Griffith, with Sevilla guide Concepción Delgado (right)

ahead to catch the next shot before it was gone. Rounding out the crew was Dan Larsen, who served as second cameraman, assisted me in scheduling decisions and shot choices, captured many beautiful still photos, helped shape the story lines, and buoyed everyone with his cheerful nature.

Over five days we captured parade after parade—and the cumulative effect became otherworldly. We moved between euphoria at witnessing such a passionate spectacle, to exhaustion at the crowds and sensory overload. Once, just when we were about to collapse, a tiny five-year-old "penitent" in his white robe and floppy cone hat stretched out his hand and offered us a lemon candy—and we carried on.

Concepción patiently explained how the various statues of the Virgin Mary captured different aspects of her sorrow, and predicted that, over the week, I would find one Mary who would speak to me personally. And so I did. Having recently been touched

continued on next page

Val with guides Marijan Kriškovič (left) and Anja Cuznar (far right), and cameraman Dan Larsen

Cameraman Peter Rummel

cont'd from previous page

by the sorrow of a friend, I bonded with the Mary of Solitude, and I left Sevilla with a picture of La Soledad in my wallet.

Our next assignment, Slovenia, was as quiet and pastoral as Spain had been hot and passionate. Slovenia's Easter festivities unfurled at a leisurely pace, in remote half-timbered villages, among sweet and shy people—scenes right out of a Grimm's fairy tale.

And it was cold. I'd packed for Sevilla's orange blossoms, but Slovenia was still in winter's grip. I layered up in T-shirts, tights, jeans, and scarves—even a pair of socks on my hands. But with the cold came a raw beauty in the early spring awakening that would translate well on film.

Our guide was the wonderful and intrepid Marijan Krišković. He took us to Slovenia's remote corners where rituals have been preserved by their isolation. Marijan introduced us to an old farmer who looked like Rumpelstiltskin—rough-hewn but elegant, with a long silver beard and a roguish twinkle. He offered us homebrewed apricot liqueur, and showed us the basket of homegrown foods he was taking to church to be blessed for Easter.

We wrapped up the shoot with Skofja Loka's traditional Passion Play. An icy wind swept off the Julian Alps. As my crew moved around filming, I sat alone in the audience—as cold as I've ever been. Eventually the old woman beside me pulled a wool blanket from her bag, and wrapped it around the two of us. We snuggled together for the rest of the performance. I will never forget that Passion Play—a haunting theatrical experience—and how cold it was that day. But my strongest memory of Easter in Slovenia will always be of an old woman's kindness.

WRAPPING UP THE FILM SHOOT—
EASTER SUNDAY

We hurried back to Rome, looking forward to putting a majestic bow on the show with a grand Easter Sunday at the Vatican. Now, Romans claim that if Palm Sunday is sunny, Easter Sunday will be miserable. It was raining. The weather was so bad that—even though we had the hard-won permission to film the Mass on St. Peter's Square—we bailed. Plan B. We spent Easter Sunday careening from venerable basilica to basilica looking for High Church pageantry. After filming four Easter Sunday Masses, we had to conclude that Rome simply doesn't celebrate Easter Sunday with much visual joy.

Fortunately, I knew we'd be in Greece for a second shot at Easter Sunday a week later. We flew to Greece for our second Holy Week in a fortnight. From Athens, we drove two hours south to Nafplio. Our charming guide, Patti Staikou,

TV production tip: Get to know the priest well before getting out the camera.

made us feel at home in her hometown. She led us to some beautiful moments—a godmother and her godchild dyeing eggs, a private choir performance, and villagers dancing around their church.

For Holy Saturday, we attended the Orthodox service. Thankfully, the priest, whose name was Dionysus, was happy to give us complete access as he performed the many rituals of this most important holiday in the Greek calendar.

Patti made sure we got a full serving of a Greek Easter Sunday. We ended up in a Greek village. I looked around me—a partying family, dancing and singing, gathered around a lamb roasting on a spit—a scene I nicknamed "My Big Fat Greek Easter." It was the ideal setting. With the entire village dancing behind me, I stood before the camera and said: "I've always enjoyed how exploring other cultures brings more meaning to my own cherished traditions. I hope this holiday journey has given new dimensions to your Easter as it has mine. I'm Rick Steves. Thanks for joining us, and Happy Easter!"

It was the perfect wrap to our filming.

POST-PRODUCTION

The next phase of the project came when we returned in spring of 2015 with lots of great footage. That's when our talented video editor, Steve Cammerano, stepped in. Steve has edited every Rick Steves episode and television special that we have produced since 2000.

The editing process for our shows is very streamlined. Whereas a big-budget reality show (like the Kardashians) shoots 60 hours of footage for each minute that makes the cut, we shoot 16 minutes for each minute that appears on our show. The Kardashians use 150 editors in large studios to comb through all that footage and piece it into order. We have one editor—Steve. One guy in a dark and humble room tucked away in our office in Edmonds, WA.

Steve had to sort through hours of raw footage (which he organizes on an

AVID edit system) and eventually fit it into 56 minutes. For example, we brought home much more Carnival craziness than we had time for. We figured about eight minutes of that, to show the pre-Christian roots of Easter, would be about right.

Steve cuts-and-pastes the footage together, following the written script. He's become so familiar with my writing and mannerisms that he sometimes subs in his own writing and voice during the edit process. Steve artfully adds music, and pieces things together in a way that gives the show a pace and emotional tone. Most of all, he's telling a story. Steve's technical knowledge of editing coupled with his respect for narrative makes a show that's informational, entertaining, and a work of art.

THIS BOOK

Gene Openshaw, lead author of this book

Having this book about Easter gave us a broader canvas to explore still more traditions, more countries, and more in-depth history.

Gene Openshaw—who has co-authored many of my books—wrote most of this book. Gene also helped generate the initial TV script, particularly the show's overall narrative arc.

The many beautiful photos that illustrate this book come from many sources (see the copyright page), but special mention goes to Elena Bauer and Dan Larson, who took time during the filming to take some still photographs. Some other photos are "screen-captures"—a still image extracted (rather laboriously) from the video. Rick's Art Director, Rhonda Pelikan, chose the images (with the help of Sandra Hundacker, Graphics Specialist) and designed the cover and layout. Designers Gopa & Ted2 and our publisher, Avalon Travel, brought it all together beautifully.

We hope you've enjoyed this book. And remember, you can watch the TV show as well. For schedule details, contact your local public television station. For more information or to stream the one-hour program anytime on your computer, see the TV corner at Ricksteves.com.

The "Making Of" this book and public television show has been a two-year journey. In bringing this story to you, we traveled from passionate Sevilla to the remote towns of Slovenia; from the stately Vatican in Rome and rustic villages of Tuscany to the Eastern-flavored rituals of Greece. Along the way, we incorporated many dimensions of Easter. We joined Roman lovers hiding necklaces in chocolate eggs, Sienese seniors singing with preschool choirs, and Sevillanos carrying floats adorned with beloved statues. We saw the epic story of Easter build with anticipation, through the Passion of Jesus to the fireworks, feasts, and "He is risen" joy of Easter Sunday.

Exploring the rich mix of European traditions, we gained fascinating insights into the Easter festivities we know and love today and wove them into a special package we hope will be enjoyed for years to come.

Buona Pasqua, Feliz Pascua, Καλό Πάσχα, Vesele velikonočne praznike, and Happy Easter!

PHOTO CREDITS

Avalon Travel
a member of the Perseus Books Group
1700 Fourth Street
Berkeley, CA 94710

Printed in Canada by Friesens
First published March 2016

ISBN 978-1-63121-359-5

For the latest on Rick Steves' lectures, guide-books, tours, public radio show, and public television series, contact:
Rick Steves' Europe, 130 Fourth Avenue North, Edmonds, WA 98020, 425/771-8303, www.ricksteves.com, rick@ricksteves.com

RICK STEVES' EUROPE
Writer: Gene Openshaw
Editors: Risa Laib, Suzanne Kotz
Editorial & Production Assistant: Jessica Shaw
Art Director & Cover Design: Rhonda Pelikan
Maps & Graphics: David C. Hoerlein,
Sandra Hundacker

AVALON TRAVEL
Senior Editor and Series Manager: Madhu Prasher
Editor: Jamie Andrade
Associate Editor: Sierra Machado
Copy Editor: Maggie Ryan
Proofreader: Rachel Feldman
Production & Typesetting: Gopa & Ted2, Inc.
Cover Design: Rhonda Pelikan, Gopa & Ted2, Inc

If you liked this book, you'll love...

Rick Steves' European Easter DVD

Sit back and enjoy Rick's one-hour public television special—
or give it as a gift—whenever you want. Filmed on location across
Spain, Italy, Switzerland, Slovenia and Greece, this DVD takes you
on a journey through local European traditions, from the raucous
parties of Carnival and the austerity of Lent to the sacred events
of Holy Week and Easter. Exploring the rich and fascinating mix
of traditions from its pagan roots to its glorious finale, *Rick Steves'
European Easter* brings a new light to this venerable holiday.

Rick Steves' European Christmas Gift Set

Experience Christmas with Rick Steves in England, Norway,
France, Italy, Germany, Austria, and Switzerland!
On your choice of DVD or Blu-ray, you get
the beautifully-filmed, hour-long *Rick Steves'
European Christmas* TV special, with 45
minutes of content you won't find in the TV
version. The 240-page companion book is
packed with thoughtful insights, colorful photos,
and more than a dozen recipes. Completing your
Christmas package, the CD includes 20 musical
selections from the TV special, giving you the
perfect soundtrack for your own holiday festivities!

Find these and other titles at ricksteves.com